Jonathan Tobelm

W9-CAP-822

BARRIERS TO
CHRISTIAN BELIEF

BARRIERS TO CHRISTIAN BELIEF

by

LEONARD GRIFFITH

B.A., B.D., D.D.

THE CITY TEMPLE, LONDON

HARPER & ROW, PUBLISHERS

New York and Evanston

BARRIERS TO CHRISTIAN BELIEF Copyright © 1961, 1962 by Leonard Griffith. Printed in the United States of America. All rights reserved. No part of this book may be used or reproduced in any manner whatsoever without written permission except in the case of brief quotations embodied in critical articles and reviews. For information address Harper & Row, Publishers, Incorporated, 49 East 33rd Street, New York 16, N. Y.

FIRST EDITION

LIBRARY OF CONGRESS CATALOG CARD NUMBER: 63-7605

Dedicated to
ANNE and MARY
whose childlike faith
has yet to encounter obstacles

CONTENTS

AUTHOR'S PREFACE

WHEN the scene of my Christian ministry changed from Canada to England, it quickly became evident to me that the burden of my preaching and writing must now be apologetic, in the classical sense of that word. Whereas in North America people are asking, "What light does the Church's Gospel shed on the practical problems of life?", in Britain, as in all of Europe, they are asking, "Is the Church's Gospel still true?" Very early in my ministry at the City Temple I preached two series of Sunday evening sermons on the general theme, *Obstacles to Christian Belief*, and was so heartened by the response of the congregation, composed largely of young people, that I felt impelled to commit the substance of this series to writing, hoping that it would find its way into the hands of many people who, though not habitual church-goers, are willing to spend time with a book which attempts to answer some of their questions about the Christian Faith. I have been encouraged to do this by Mr. Leonard Cutts, Religious Book Editor of Hodder and Stoughton, and for his friendship and advice I am deeply indebted. Thanks are due also to my competent secretary, Miss Winifred Haddon, whose long association with my distinguished predecessor, Dr. Leslie Weatherhead, has made her an expert in the preparation of manuscripts, and to Miss Joyce Burrell, Editor of *The City Temple Tidings*, for reading the proofs. In addition to the usual footnote acknowledgments, I make special reference to a book which fifty years ago dealt far more exhaustively and capably with the same theme, R. F. Horton's *My Belief*.[1] I make no claim to originality. Others have laboured, and I have entered into the fruits of their labours, and my highest gratitude lies only in the desire to be a worthy steward of the Christian heritage.

A.L.G.

[1] Fleming H. Revell Company, New York 1909.

The New Scepticism

"There were thousands of us in the pews at the City Temple yesternoon, and one man was in the pulpit. We had come from warehouses and offices, from banks and shops, from the Exchange and the markets, giving up our dinner-hour, and taking our snack of food when or where or how we could, so that a higher purpose was duly served. And what had we come out for to hear? Simply Carlyle's 'Speaking Man'."

— *The Daily Telegraph*, 1903

THIS "Speaking Man" was Reginald John Campbell, the young, brilliant, controversial successor to Joseph Parker in the ministry of London's famous City Temple. For more than thirty years Parker had made his pulpit-throne a bastion of Christian orthodoxy. Once, indeed, he had thundered forth magisterially that if anything but the historic Gospel were ever proclaimed within the City Temple, the name *Ichabod* should be written in bold letters across the entrance. In literal fact, some unknown prankster was soon to perform this very act of defamation, because Parker's mantle had fallen on the shoulders of a theological liberal whose persuasive and scholarly exposition of "The New Theology" convulsed the religious world and brought upon his head the wrath of his conservative brethren in all the churches. Newspapers quoted his every word, sophisticated men discussed his sermons on the streets and in their clubs and offices, and each Thursday at noon thousands of busy people sacrificed their precious lunch-hour and joined the vast crowds that thronged into the City Temple to hear this handsome, silvery-voiced man of God preach for sixty minutes on the deepest issues of the Christian Faith.

Our imagination would be hard-pressed to reconstruct such a scene in the City Temple or in any other church today. Some of these elements might be present at a modern mid-week service of worship, but not the great, eager congregation, not the tense atmosphere of expectancy, and certainly not the willingness to listen to an hour-long dissertation on theology.

People are frankly no longer concerned about the ever-lasting arguments between theologians; for the most part they have not the interest or the time to be interested in what Christian scholars are trying to say. Controversy in other realms of thought fascinates them, and they consider it their duty to keep abreast and be able to talk intelligently on the current disputes between the scientists or the economists. They are quick to take sides on the latest government budget or the most recent foreign policy or the current Test Match or football scores, because these are the things that really matter to them. Theology, on the other hand, is *passé*; it bores them; it no longer seems important or relevant.

Even within the Church today a vastly different situation confronts the preacher than that which confronted R. J. Campbell half a century ago. Campbell's generation had the supreme advantage of speaking to an age of faith, an age that still believed in the basic Christian doctrines, and at the very least he could assume a modicum of theological literacy on which to build. One of his contemporaries said recently, however, that whereas in any congregation sixty years ago you could count on a general sense of guilt, now the only thing you can count on is a general sense of doubt. After spending some time in Europe, an American theological professor concluded that today the preacher can expect two reactions to every sermon, "Oh Yeah!" and "So What?" Never has Christian orthodoxy been more sharply challenged. Whereas in previous years the Church could build its theological structure on certain widely-accepted postulates, today no postulates are granted and no maxims go unchallenged. No longer is it a matter of measuring one theory of the Atonement against other theories of the Atonement, but rather of convincing people that such a thing as the Atonement ever took place at all. In any effectual presentation of its Gospel the Church must start at the beginning, taking nothing for granted and making no assumptions whatever.

This is no cynical judgment but a realistic observation of fact. Lecturing to the students in a theological college, the author of this book attempted to outline the philosophical reasons for our Christian belief in immortality. I spoke of the instinct for immortality which the Creator has implanted in his children, an instinct, surely, that will not deceive us. I spoke about the universality of this belief, its acceptance by all civilizations and by the intellectual giants of every age. I added the moral consideration that only on the basis of hope in a future life do the injustices and inequalities of this life make sense. At this point an eager-faced student, dissatisfied with what seemed like an unbiblical and sub-christian presentation of the theme, interrupted and asked impatiently, "But, sir, does not the Church accept all of these arguments?" "That depends," I replied, "on how you define the Church. These arguments are certainly implicit in the historic Christian creeds which go far beyond them, but do not make the mistake of identifying the Church with the historic Christian creeds. The Church is made up of people, and people must be convinced afresh in every generation."

In large areas of the world, some of them the former strongholds of Christianity, the majority of people stand outside the orthodox community of faith altogether. They may be of the upper classes who retain their ancestral connection with the Church only for the sake of social respectability. They may be intellectuals, in which case they wear a garment of agnosticism, believing that the world expects them to wear it. They may be labourers, belonging to that lost province of Christianity with which the Church has almost completely lost touch. Or they may be of the new bourgeoisie, excited by their growing affluence, but utterly materialistic in their thinking and so indifferent to the Church that they have even forgotten the name of the Church they stay away from. In attempting to reach them, the Church confronts a spiritual hostility inferior even to that of the most primitive tribes in Central Africa. These are the true pagans in the accepted and classical sense of that word. They no longer believe, if they ever did believe, the simplest rudiments of Christian doctrine.

It would be a superficial and utterly false appraisal of the situation to explain the spiritual illiteracy of modern man in terms either of ignorance or indifference. If enlightenment were the requisite of faith, then Christianity should have entered its Golden Age, because never has the general level of enlightenment among all classes of people been higher. Nor can we accuse the modern pagan of merely ignoring the claims of Christianity, because the truth is that he has examined these claims, sometimes more critically than we give him credit for doing, and having measured them against his own needs and the needs of the world in which he lives, he has reached, perhaps reluctantly, the conclusion that Christianity no longer has the answer to those needs.

In a study booklet prepared by the World Council of Churches we read this sobering paragraph:

"Christianity throughout the world is facing a crisis as great as any which has come upon it in the course of its history. In the past hundred years every one of its traditional foundations has been exposed to the most searching criticism. Christians are being compelled to face challenges to their basic beliefs which seem greater even than those in the time of the Renaissance and the Reformation. Large numbers of people in both East and West are convinced that modern man has outgrown religion altogether. A new kind of secularism has developed which considers the Christian faith as outdated and unintelligible. Any real concern with God is discarded as irrelevant. Many consider this attitude a kind of liberation. Some put their hope in science. Others simply accept what they call the absurdities of life, and many are lost in meaninglessness and despair."

There is a new scepticism abroad in the world today, which is inevitable in an age of revolution when every sphere of thought and action — science, politics, industry, culture — has undergone such rapid change. Under the storm of political and technological upheaval many of the old landmarks have been swept away, and men have felt compelled to re-examine their own traditionally-accepted values. With no disrespect for the simple faith of their fathers, they cannot help feeling that their fathers, living in an uncomplicated and unscientific age, may possibly have oversimplified life and been content with an explanation of life which no longer covers the facts. To be sure, believing Christians have staked their lives on the reality of God and the Saviourhood of Christ and the Gospel of redemption and the hope of eternity, but a mistake is no less a mistake even though it may be compounded over a period of nineteen centuries.

There has never been a scarcity of intellectuals who insist that the meaning of life can be found in purely materialistic

14

values and who dedicate themselves with messianic fervour to the debunking of those spiritual values which have their rootage in the Gospel of Jesus Christ, but somehow these iconoclasts seem more prolific today, and ordinary people seem more willing to listen to them. Society has not dispensed with its High Priests; it has merely transferred the mantle of authority from the prophet to the scientist, the economist, the journalist and the practical man of affairs. These have become the spokesmen of our culture; they smile benignly from the television screen like a schoolmaster patiently instructing his class along the path to mental maturity. They do not deny the reality of ultimate questions, nor do they doubt the extremity of need inherent in human nature and society, but they do insist that the ultimate answers to these questions and these needs must be found elsewhere than in the Christian Faith. "The time has come," they assert, "for this magnificent, two-legged creature called 'Man', this crown and flower of the evolutionary process, to break loose from the painfully irrational and restrictive discipline of religious superstition. For too long he has lived in a state of adolescence and pauperism. Now he must grow up and become Man in the mature sense of that word. He must learn to stand on his own feet, work out his own salvation, assume control of his own destiny and be his own god."

There is nothing new about this humanistic insistence that the way of maturity is the way of irreligion — it goes back to the Garden of Eden — but scepticism in our day does have this novel feature, that it has migrated from the ivory tower to the road. In a less sophisticated manner the average man on the street echoes the cynicism of his intellectual superiors and views with profound distrust the claims of historic Christianity. Not that he regards the impending demise of religion with any feelings of elation, because when all the outworn clichés have been spoken about the failure of Christianity to answer his questions about life and the universe, the fact remains that those questions are still there to plague and torment him. He may care nothing for what seem to him like decadent theories of sin and salvation, but he does care about the worth of his own life and that of his fellows beyond eating, sleeping, working, procreating and dying. However inarticulately, he wants release from the tyranny of his own anxieties and passions and from the mass social forces that sweep him headlong from one catastrophe to another. As he sees it, Christianity has had its chance and failed; it simply does not have the answers. But if someone could show him that Christianity does have the answers, if the claims of the Church could be re-presented to him reasonably and persuasively, he might be willing to rethink those claims and reconsider his relationship to historic Christianity.

This book is written out of the conviction that many people who today stand outside the orthodox community of faith do so neither from antagonism nor indifference, but from an honest inability to accept the Church's Gospel. They are not proud to be classed among the sceptics. They do not enjoy their unbelief and they derive no morbid satisfaction from the prospect of the Church diminishing in influence as rival secular faiths bid imperiously for the allegiance of men. These are open-minded people, willing to be convinced. They respect Christian certitude wherever they find it, and they would give anything to be delivered from their state of nihilism because they know that, despite the preachments of the humanists, man cannot stand on his own feet or work out his own salvation. Man is a creature, infinitesimally small and weak in relation to his environment, and if he would live successfully within that environment, then he must have something to which he can cling, some wisdom, some power that is older, greater and stronger than himself. There are people today who honestly *want* to believe that the Gospel of Jesus Christ has the answer to the world's problems and to their own problems, and they *would* believe, except that the path to belief seems blocked by insuperable obstacles of a theoretical and practical nature. If these obstacles could be removed or scaled or in any way circumvented, then many who stand hesitatingly on the threshold of spiritual pilgrimage might take the venture of faith and move forward to at least a tentative acceptance of the Christian position.

The cardinal task confronting the Church in the fulfilment of its evangelistic mission is the task of apologetics. With gentleness and reverence the Church "must always be prepared to make a strong defence to anyone who calls it to account for the hope that is in it". Half a century ago we could speak confidently about the foolishness of fighting battles which were already won, but the world has changed in fifty years, and a Church that is alive to the exigencies of the human situation will know that in the struggle for the minds of men it must address itself to the scepticism that possesses the minds of men and be prepared to fight those battles as if they had never been fought before.

With weapons of sweet reasonableness and loving constraint such a battle has been joined in the pages of this book. I am certain that while many of the obstacles that block the road to Christian Faith are genuine enough, they are not insuperable; indeed they remain obstacles only because we have never assaulted them with all the powers of our God-given intelligence. If we could apply to the problems of the spiritual life the same faculty of concentration that we apply to the purely academic and practical problems, we should find that many barriers to belief, if not entirely illusory, are based on astonishingly insecure foundations. This book renews the gracious invitation of that Hebrew prophet who said on behalf of God, "Come now, let us reason together . . ." With unbiased minds, stripped of all irrational prejudices, let us face up frankly and courageously to some of the worst spectres of doubt.

Because the following chapters have been written from the perspective of the Christian Faith, two basic presuppositions run through them like a thread: first, that the means of eliminating or surmounting the most formidable obstacles to Christian belief lies in a new and deeper study of the Bible; second, that Jesus Christ is Lord, and that though men may refuse to hear him, he still exercises Lordship over them and still speaks the one Word of healing. As these lines are being written, the eyes of Christian people turn towards New Delhi in India, soon to be the scene of the Third Assembly of the World Council of Churches which will take as its theme that most extraordinary claim of Christ, "I am the light of the world". Extraordinary as it may be, however, Christ continues to make it. People try to forget about him, but sooner or later the claim is renewed. The purpose of this book will be achieved if through its pages the living Christ confronts men, shedding his own light into the darkness of their doubt.

I

Faith in Honest Doubt

"I THINK I must be an atheist!" The lady who spoke made that statement in all sincerity. She had always been a religious woman, always attended church, always believed what Christians are supposed to believe, but now for the first time in her life the cold fingers of doubt gripped her mind, and she found herself questioning the very faith that she had taken for granted since childhood. Nor was it a mere academic doubt, that rather smug and blasé scepticism that becomes fashionable at the close of one's first year at university. This woman's doubt chilled her soul like a prolonged fit of melancholy, and inwardly she felt ashamed and sinful and terrified lest her mood communicate itself to her husband and her growing boys. In sheer desperation she confided to a close friend, "I still go to church, you know. I try to keep up appearances, but I just can't believe any more. It's terrible to lose your religious faith. I think I must be an atheist."

Unless he absolutely pigeon-holes his religious belief, so as to keep it separate from other departments of his life, the intelligent, sensitive Christian cannot help these days being haunted by doubts. There is so much in the modern world that challenges the naïve and optimistic faith of the nineteenth century, so much in the struggles of human life that makes belief in a wise and good God difficult. Some of our doubts have theoretical causes. We see how science has pushed back the frontiers of knowledge, so that what appeared mysterious and supernatural to past generations appears perfectly explainable and natural to us, and we cannot help asking ourselves whether, as man gains increasing mastery over the universe, he will not eliminate the supernatural from life altogether. Other doubts have more practical causes, the sort voiced by a modern playwright: "If God is God, he is not good; if God is good, he is not God"—which means that God either has not the love or he has not the power to resolve a human situation in which there

19

is more misery, more injustice and more innocent suffering than at any period since the world began. It would be strange indeed if Christians living realistically in the twentieth century, this age of science and sputniks, of cold war and hydrogen bombs, of revolutions and rising nationalisms, did not find the simple faith of their childhood challenged by doubts.

The Bible has much to say on the problem of doubt, but one thing in particular. It tells us not to be ashamed of our doubts or even afraid of them. It is not sinful to doubt; the real sin consists in the docile and unthinking acceptance of a mass of antiquated dogmas, in pretending to be sure where we are not sure. When a man accepts the Christian Faith unquestioningly, when he says quite calmly that he has never had a doubt, then it is a sure sign that he has crucified his intelligence and settled down to a case of hardening of the spiritual arteries. This book is written for the encouragement of someone who may be struggling with his unbelief. To such a person the Bible says: "By all means put the Gospel to the test of your doubts; any Gospel that will not stand up to them is not worth believing anyway." God does not want any man to accept or pretend to accept what he cannot believe. We come closer to God through honest unbelief than we do through dishonest belief. What the Bible teaches on the problem of doubt has been summarized in one of the poems of Tennyson, "There lives more faith in honest doubt, Believe me, than in half the creeds."

In the Bible the great believers are the great doubters. The writer of the seventy-third Psalm came to sublime faith in God's presence and sufficiency for this life and the next, "Whom have I in heaven but thee? and there is none on earth that I desire beside thee," but he came to that faith through the painful process of doubt, "As for me, my feet were almost gone; my steps had well nigh slipped." The prophet Jeremiah counsels his people to glory not in might, wisdom or riches, but in the Lord; and in almost the same breath he curses the day of his birth, "Woe is me, my mother that made me, a man of strife and contention to the whole land." Paul declares that he is persuaded that nothing can separate him from the love of Christ, but writing of his sufferings and trials, he says, "We were so utterly, unbearably crushed that we despaired of life itself."

The saints were men of doubt as well as faith. There was

a time in the life of John Knox, the Scottish Reformer, when his soul knew "anger, wrath and indignation, which it conceived against God, calling all his promises in doubt". We sing Luther's rugged hymn, "A mighty fortress is our God," and we suppose that he never questioned his faith, but we see him so gloomy and despondent that once, in order to shake him out of it, his wife dressed in deep mourning, and in answer to Luther's question she replied, "I am mourning the death of God. From the way you are behaving, God must surely be dead." At Tintern Abbey the poet Wordsworth could write,

> "I have felt
> A presence that disturbs me with the joy
> Of elevated thoughts . . ."

But in the frightening, disillusioning aftermath of the French Revolution he cried out,

> "I lost
> All feeling of conviction, and, in fine,
> Sick, wearied out with contrarities,
> Yielded up moral questions in despair."

So often we envy a man for the certainty of his faith. Calm, serene, confident, he seems to us as immovable as the Rock of Gibraltar; but that shows how little we know about him, because if we could get behind that placid exterior, we should be astonished at the fierceness of his inner struggle. Ministers who preach to their congregations week after week must give the impression of being very dogmatic creatures, very sure of themselves, protected by their pulpits and insulated by their clerical collars against the doubts which assail other men in the arena of work and business. "He has to be sure," one layman said of his minister. "If *he* begins to doubt, that leaves the rest of us with nothing to hang on to." Yet that is exactly the struggle that every minister fights, the struggle to preserve and deepen his faith in those eternal realities which justify his very vocation as God's representative before men. Sometimes he may become discouraged and lose the struggle. What that means has been expressed in a recently-published poem:

> "Sooner or later the preacher
> Wakes up to the fact
> That he can't save *everybody*.

21

He may even think
That after all,
There *is* such a division
As the Elect.

If he goes on thinking
He may come to realize
That the 'Elect' are inclined
To agree with him.

If by some chance
He contemplates still further,
He may find
That *some* of the Damned
Have a *point*.

Then he may wonder
If *anyone at all* can be saved!
He might even count himself
Among the great mass
Of the Lost!

He will then flounder about
Snatching at slivers of truth.

He may even discover
That he can't swim."[1]

So let us reckon with the fact that religious faith has its
moods, its high moods of great assurance and its low moods
when confidence sags and trust is insecure. Let us not con-
ceive of the Christian life as a life of uninterrupted progress,
like the journey of a mountaineer who climbs steadily up-
ward, never looking back, conquering one fresh peak after
another. Faith is an undulating journey that traverses not
only mountain-tops and level plains but also deep valleys
from which the certainty of God seems to have vanished. The
weather of the mind and spirit varies, ranging from sunlight
through dense fog to pitch darkness, and there are times
when we stumble through that darkness unsure that anyone
or anything is there. The Apostle James has oversimplified
the situation when he contrasts the man of doubt with the

[1] "Death of Another Salesman", by Thomas C. Arthur. Published in *The Christian Century*, 1961.

man of faith, describing the doubter as "a heaving sea ruffled by the wind", a "double minded man" to whom the Lord cannot give anything. We are not men of faith or men of doubt, but a mixture of both. Every one of us wanting to be sure of God must say what the man in the Gospel story said to Jesus, "Lord, I believe; help thou mine unbelief!"

We shall not deal with our doubts by ignoring them. A popular novelist makes one of his characters say every time she runs up against a perplexing problem, "I shall think about that tomorrow." So do we try to handle our doubts — by silencing them as we would silence a barking dog and by going on with our practice of religion as if they did not exist. The trouble, however, is that we have not dealt with our doubts but only repressed them, only driven them down into the recesses of our subconscious minds where they fester and gather strength and eventually erupt in sheer unbelief and cynicism. Any kind of illness, physical, psychological or spiritual, should be dealt with in its earliest stages, and the time to deal with soul-sickness is not in the advanced paralysis of agnosticism and atheism, but in its infancy when those little, minor, irritating symptoms of doubt first begin to appear.

Therefore the wise man will not repress his doubts but will force them out into the open and will calmly and squarely face up to them. He will reckon with the fact that a great deal of his uncertainty about religious truth may be rooted in himself and especially in his imperfect understanding of religious truth. In his little book, *Invitation to Pilgrimage*,[1] the late John Baillie says, "It has been my own lot to be constantly involved in discussion with men who feel unable to identify themselves with the faith and outlook of the Christian Church . . . And it is seldom, if ever, that I have felt that their doubts were denials to be based on a true understanding of what they were doubting or denying." He adds, "Men criticize and even oppose Christianity without ever having taken much trouble to discover what it is all about . . . It is remarkable what nonsense is spoken about it even by men of the highest distinction in departmental fields of knowledge . . ."

Sometimes our doubts have emotional causes. That was the case with Thomas who was absent from the Upper Room

[1] John Baillie, *Invitation to Pilgrimage* (Pelican Book), pp. 17–19.

on Easter evening when the risen Christ appeared to the disciples, who later doubted the testimony of his friends, and for whose benefit Christ came again to the Upper Room, showing him the wounds in his hands and side. Thomas said, "Unless I see . . . I will not believe," and though it seems like the argument of a stubborn sceptic, yet when you read the New Testament and piece together what scattered fragments of information we have about this doubting disciple, you realize that Thomas was not a sceptic but a pessimist. The Cross struck a mortal blow at every hope that he had ever cherished, and nothing, not even the radiant good news that his Master had risen, could retrieve him from the abyss of his melancholy and gloom. Unlike people who enjoy their doubt rather flippantly, Thomas felt wretched about it. He wanted to believe. He would have given anything to be certain that Jesus was really alive. His was not the doubt of reasoned argument but the doubt of a great sorrow.

It is also possible that our doubts may be rooted in moral difficulties. Not reason, but sin prevents a great many people from believing. They are taken captive by the lusts of the flesh and the lusts of the eyes and the vainglory of life, and they cannot afford to pay the price that believing would involve. They salve their souls and mollify their consciences by pretending to be baffled by the complexities of theology; they throw up a smokescreen of calculated doubt to camouflage their moral deficiencies; theirs is the doubt of an uneasy conscience. When a person says, "I am having trouble with the Apostles' Creed," one is tempted to reply, "I suspect that your real trouble is with the Ten Commandments." Many a young doubter deserves to be dealt with as Benjamin Jowett, Master of Balliol College, Oxford, dealt with an undergraduate who came to him and said, "I am having difficulty finding proof for the existence of God." Jowett snapped, "Well, young man, you had better find God by five o'clock this afternoon, or you will have to leave this college."

But that does not dispose of the problem. All these considerations aside, we have genuine doubts rooted not in our personal peculiarities, but in objective factors that sometimes beat with hurricane force on the frail structure of our belief. Let us get one thing clear, we shall not manage our doubts simply by surrendering to them and by giving up the struggle.

Arthur John Gossip once wrote, "Some people, when belief comes hard, fling away from the Christian faith altogether. But in heaven's name," he asked, speaking himself from the depths of personal disaster, "fling away to what?" The torment of doubt is no time to divorce ourselves from the fellowship and the resources of religious faith, no time to cease praying and throw away the Bible and turn our backs on the Church. Doubts torment us not because we have too much religion but too little, and then, if ever, is the time to intensify the spiritual life, to pray with greater earnestness, read the Bible with renewed concentration, involve ourselves more deeply in the fellowship of other Christians, and cast ourselves with greater humility and dependence upon the enlightening grace of God.

Harry Emerson Fosdick entitles a memorable sermon, "The Importance of Doubting Your Doubts". He begins with the proposition that the capacity to doubt is one of man's noblest powers. The great servants of the race have been men who in the face of universally accepted falsehoods dared to stand up and say, "I doubt that!" Christian theology has been delivered from some of its worst crudities by daring men of doubt. Augustine was a doubter, so were Martin Luther and John Wesley and Karl Barth and Reinhold Niebuhr. The great believers are all the great doubters, great because they did not stop with their unbelief but carried it to its logical conclusion until at last they saw the untenability of their own doubts and seriously began to doubt them. In *Invitation to Pilgrimage* John Baillie says that he is happy to count among his friends a number of men of high intellectual distinction who have returned to the full Christian outlook after years of defection from it, and he says that in practically every case the renewed hospitality of their minds to Christian truth came about through their awakening to the essential untenability of the alternative position which they had been previously tempted to occupy. These were open-minded men who did not rest their unbelief on a structure of prejudice and ignorance, but viewed it impartially and, having carried it through to its logical conclusion, went beyond it and began to doubt even their own doubts.

There was a D. Ph. student at Oxford who came away from his supervisor's office feeling terribly despondent. The supervisor told him that he had read all the English literature on his subject and that he would now have to read the untranslated works of German scholars. "But, sir," the student protested, "I don't know German." "Then it would seem," said the supervisor matter-of-factly, "that you will have to take time out to learn it. You have gone as far as you can go otherwise." God says something like that to us in our doubts: "My child, you and I have gone as far as we can go together on your present level of spiritual understanding. Therefore I am withdrawing myself from you for a time. When you have wrestled a bit, and prayed and studied and deepened your understanding of Christian truth, then we shall come together again and move forward."

It is not the worst thing that can happen to a Christian believer that he should fall into a period of spiritual slump and begin questioning the religious truths that he has always taken for granted. This turmoil of doubt may be the surest sign that he has graduated from Sunday School and begun to think for himself and is advancing from a second-hand to a first-hand experience of Christianity. We need not be ashamed of our doubts any more than we need to be ashamed of the growing pains of adolescence. Honesty, humility and a large dose of scepticism towards neat little theories do not exclude a person from faith; on the contrary, they are the prerequisites for reaching a faith that is more stable and mature.

There is faith in honest doubt. That is the essential message of the Book of *Job*, the moving story of a righteous and godly man who, despite his righteousness and godliness, suffered cruel calamities. Even when Job shrieked his blasphemies against heaven, God preferred him to his three "comforters", the representatives of Jewish orthodoxy. Why? Because Job was not afraid to doubt, not afraid to break with a religious faith which no longer answered his questions. In the face of these questions about the suffering of an innocent man Job's "comforters" retreated to their "Maginot Line" and dug themselves in. They sang, "The old-time religion was good enough for father, and it's good enough for me." But not good enough for Job. As he saw it, the old-time religion had proved inadequate to the facts of life; it had been weighed in the balances and found wanting. So where the "comforters" remained stuck in the mud of traditionalism, Job moved on to the higher ground of new insight into a world of thought and emotion whence they could not follow. They had theology, but Job had God. They had the little answers, but Job had the big questions, and there was more honest religion in his questions than in their answers. Job blasphemed, to be sure, but it was the blasphemy of a new and more realistic faith struggling to be born, an agony of doubt that took him nearer to heaven than his friends with their dust-covered dogmatism could ever attain.

That is the message of the Bible; it says, in effect: don't be ashamed of doubt; welcome it as a sure sign that the Holy Spirit is at work in your life, compelling you to discard religious beliefs which ought to be discarded because they do not answer the questions that men are asking today. You have not only a capacity to doubt; you have a duty to doubt if you would grow into an understanding of God that will meet the needs of your own life and the life of the world in this changing and totally unpredictable mid-twentieth century.

What of the meantime, however? We may assure a hospital patient that when he is recovered he can look forward to renewed health and strength, but how do we comfort him now in the weakness and agony of his post-operative pains when his morale sinks below zero and secretly he wishes that he could die? To be sure, the Bible gives us hope that we can look beyond our doubts to a more stable and mature faith, but in the wretchedness of our doubt we are not interested in the future; we can only think about the present. What comfort does the Bible offer us here and now?

This final question brings us into the presence of Jesus. We must think of his struggle in Gethsemane as supremely a struggle with the doubts in his own soul. As God's Son, Jesus came to earth to do battle with all those forces of evil which had proved too strong for the unaided strength of men. He came to displace the Kingdom of Satan by the Kingdom of God, and up to a point he proved his superiority. He defeated Satan in the wilderness of temptation; he scorned the tempter's voice speaking through the voices of his enemies and his friends; he broke the grip of evil's power on the bodies and souls of men. So was it now God's will that he should go to the Cross, that he who had proved himself master of the forces of darkness should suddenly capitulate

27

to the forces of darkness and allow them to conquer him in death? How could it be possible that this utter disgrace and defeat, this dramatic and decisive about-face should be the plan and purpose of God for the world's redemption? Even the Son of God wrestled with the agony of doubt. "O my father," he prayed, "if it be possible, let this cup pass from me . . ." Yet, see how he dealt with his doubt. "Nevertheless, not as I will, but as thou wilt" — by trust and obedience, by leaving to God's wisdom all that he could not understand and by going out to suffer and die on the basis of what he could understand.

That is the Christian answer to the problem of doubt. It bids us remember that while there is much about the Christian Faith that we cannot believe, there is still a great deal that we can believe, and if we will live on the basis of this, if we will trust it and be obedient to it, then God himself will enlighten our minds and impart his own truth to us as we are prepared to receive it. Doubts never resolve themselves in the ivory tower of scepticism, but only on the hard road of Christian obedience and service. Someone says, "I cannot believe the theology of the creeds." "What do you believe?" we ask him. He replies, "Well, I believe in God, and I believe that Jesus was the most godly man who ever lived and that his teachings are the finest ever given to the human race." "Then follow Jesus," we answer, "make him your Master and Lord. Trust him, obey him, and he himself will lead you to new adventures in Christian understanding."

2

Is Religion Necessary?

MANY of the people who stand outside the community of religious faith today, and many of the people who stand within it hesitatingly, do so as a matter of intellectual and moral honesty. They are not biased against religion; they are not like those who happen to have read one book by an agnostic and on the basis of it decided that twenty centuries of theology is bunk. These are intelligent people, open-minded and seeking for the truth, who would honestly like to believe that Christianity does have the answer to the world's problems and to their own problems. They wish they could accept the truth of the Gospel, but certain obstacles of an intellectual or historical or moral nature block their path, and only when these obstacles have been dealt with to their satisfaction can they move forward to take a Christian position.

Perhaps the most obvious and the most practical barrier to Christian belief is the sight of men and women in our society who seem to manage very well without it. These are charming and excellent people of the highest integrity who lead rich, complete, useful and happy lives, but lives that have no room whatever for the belief and practice of religion. They may be missing something by their crass indifference to spiritual values, but they are not conscious of it; and because they are what they are and because we like them and respect them, they constitute a stumbling-block to our own belief.

So we come to our first question: Is religion necessary at all? Many would answer with a frank "No!" They would say that religion has played a useful role in man's evolutionary development, but that man has outgrown the need for religion and that within a few generations this will be universally recognized. Other things will furnish a sufficient basis for life and thought. At the Darwin Centennial in Chicago a few years ago Sir Julian Huxley spoke of a new

29

order of thought that will eventually doom all religions. "Religions," he said, "are destined to disappear in competition with other truer and more embracing thought organizations which are handling the same range of raw or processed experience."

Miss Perkins was a little old lady who lived by herself in a large house on a busy street very near the centre of the city. She dressed in old-fashioned clothing and seemed a social anachronism in both her appearance and manner. How she manicured her garden! Especially in autumn she must have raked the fallen leaves several times a day. One thought that she sat near the window and watched them fall and then rushed out to catch them before they defiled her precious lawn. A group of doctors bought up the adjacent property with a view to erecting a large medical arts building and having next to it a sizeable parking lot. Miss Perkins's house stood squarely in the middle of this. Would she sell? She would not, for any price. In this house she had been born and in this house she intended to die. So the doctors did not argue. They put the building on one side of her and the parking lot on the other, knowing that nature would take care of the situation and that after Miss Perkins's death they could name their own price and tear the house down. Many people feel exactly that way about the Church—an old-fashioned institution to be humoured and tolerated because it is on its way out anyway. Before long it can be torn down completely to make way for a medical building, a scientific laboratory, a social agency or even a broadcasting studio. These things, after all, perform the Church's function more effectively. These things make religion unnecessary.

There was a Hebrew poet who had the courage to carry this point of view through to its logical conclusion. The writer of the fourteenth Psalm paints a graphic picture of an unreligious society. He shows us a community of men who have ceased to believe in God and who have, therefore, dropped religion as a department of human life and activity. Having shown us what life on a purely materialistic basis would be like, he allows us to draw our own conclusions and decide for ourselves whether or not religion is necessary.

Arrestingly he begins, "The fool hath said in his heart, There is no God." It seems rather strong language with

30

which to describe the practical atheist, the man who denies God for all practical purposes, yet the more we ponder it, the more we feel that the Psalmist may have used exactly the right word. We call a man a fool who denies a self-evident truth and who takes a position based on arguments that will not stand against the bar of reason and experience. For example, suppose someone told us that only the planet earth can support human life and that however far we cruise through outer space in the next decade, we shall not find anywhere in this universe another planet inhabited by living creatures. We might disagree with him; we might say that he has insufficient evidence for so sweeping a claim; but we shall not call him a fool, because we know that his claim cannot yet be proved or disproved. If, on the other hand, he tells us quite dogmatically that the islands of the Pacific cannot support human life, we shall probably call him something worse than a fool, because even a school child knows that these islands are inhabited; we send missionaries to them, we exchange correspondence with them, we have met members of the native population. No life on the Pacific Islands? Sheer foolishness to make so preposterous a claim!

In that category the Psalmist rates the man who denies the reality of God and therefore the necessity of religion. There is no point arguing with such a man, because his arguments will not stand against the bar of reason and experience. He refuses to concede self-evident facts. He pays no attention to man's history which is, after all, the history of religion. Somewhere back in the early millenniums of the evolutionary process, there emerged from the jungles and caves a creature who lifted his face from the dust and learned to say "I am". He went beyond that and learned to say "I think", and his thought has taken the atom and turned it into limitless power. He progressed still further and learned to say "I feel"; he is sensitive to ecstatic joy and to an agony which penetrates to his deepest nature. He went further still and learned to say "I ought"; he is disturbed by conscience, he feels the tug of duty. He went even beyond that to say "I love". He knows that the ultimate gesture in life is not the clenched fist but the outstretched hand. And he took a final step. He learned to say "I worship". He learned to lift his eyes and bend his knee. He learned to know God.

31

That was the climax of man's evolution and it came very early. In every age, in every civilization, primitive or highly-developed, there has been that in man's ordered life which testifies to the necessity of religion.

Man's culture reflects this need. When you go through a museum and study the relics of ancient civilizations — the art, the pottery, the burial customs, the hieroglyphics inscribed on walls — you find that most of them have a religious motif. Indeed, it is from the religion of a people that we learn most about that people. We hold up the ancient Greeks as supreme rationalists, yet who were more religious than the Greek philosophers? The Apostle Paul, walking through the streets of Athens, stumbled over the images of so many gods and goddesses, that he began his sermon on Mars Hill, "Men of Athens, I perceive that in every way you are very religious." Surveying the culture of the past two thousand years, the art, architecture, literature and music, we realize that there would not be much left if we purged it of all that men have painted, built, written and composed to the glory of God. When people cease to be moved by Handel's *Messiah*, when they cease to be thrilled by the majesty of a great cathedral, when they no longer desire their marriages solemnized and when they can bury their dead without invoking the presence of God, when they lose the sense of mystery and awe and cease to believe that what is impenetrable to them really exists, then only will they have outgrown their need for religion.

It happens sometimes that society throws out a particular kind of religion. A dictionary published behind the Iron Curtain to take care of some twenty thousand non-Russian words defines religion as "a fantastic faith in gods, angels and spirits, a faith without any scientific foundations, maintained by reactionary circles for the subjugation of working people and for building up the power of the exploiting bourgeois classes". So much for Christianity, declares Marxism. But has Marxism shown up religion to be unnecessary? On the contrary, the communist world has shown that men do not get rid of a god; they simply exchange their gods. When they throw out one religion they take up another in its place. What, in fact, *is* communism but a perverted parody of Christianity: Its one God — Dialectical Materialism; its Trinity — Marx the Lawgiver, Lenin the Incarnate

Truth, Khruschev the Guide and Comforter; its Chosen People—the Proletariat, destined to inherit the earth; its Devil—Private Property; its Church—the Communist Party; its Scriptures—the writings of Marx-Leninism; its infallible witness—the will and word of the Kremlin; its Last Judgment—the violent overthrow of Capitalism and the enthronement of the Workers; its Millennium—the withering away of the State in a classless brotherhood.

Man needs religion. Whether willing to admit it or not, he is a religious animal. Since the dawn of his consciousness he has asked certain basic questions and possessed certain basic aspirations which have found their only answer in some kind of religion. When he comes face to face with the mystery of the natural world about him, he is driven to ask, "What lies at the root of all existence? Whence has it come?" When he looks within himself and faces the mystery of his own personality, he is driven to question the strange, uncontrollable conflict of powers, good and evil. When on the crest of love and laughter he is thrown against the sheer, stark fact of tragedy, he is driven to ask, "Why has it happened? What am I going to do with it?" When he looks beyond, beyond the grave, beyond history, beyond the dead, cold world that this globe will one day become, he is driven to ask, "What lies beyond? Toward what is everything moving? Where do we go from here?" Out of these queries springs what we call the sense of religion, the sense of ultimate things, and that sense has, if anything, been deepened by the growth of civilization and the increase of scientific knowledge. Man is a religious animal. He can no more cease to be religious than he can cease to be rational. And when he ceases to be rational, what does he become but a fool? The question is not, Does man need a religion? but rather, What kind of religion is right?

The Psalmist approaches our question in yet another sense. Is religion necessary? Does it perform an indispensable function? Do we need religion as a cohesive and stabilizing force in our society? Does it act as a social conscience? Does it keep society clean? Does it preserve the higher values? Does it promote the practice of charity and increase the sense of social responsibility? There is only one way to answer that question, and that is to look at a community of

33

men who have renounced religion as a department of human life and thought and activity and have reorganized themselves on a materialistic basis. Here is a town that passes a by-law forbidding the erection of any churches, that removes from its public library any books on religious subjects, that prohibits the teaching of religion in the schools, even as an element of culture, a community of people organized on the proposition that there is no God. The Psalmist pictures this godless society, and we see it for what it is, a society without any conscience, any cohesion, progressively degraded, sinking deeper and deeper into the mire of corruption and crime. "They are corrupt, they do abominable deeds, there is none that does good. They have all gone astray, they are all alike corrupt, there is none that does good, no, not one. Have they no knowledge, all the evil doers who eat up my people as they eat bread, and do not call upon the Lord?"

Of course, the cynic will retort, "This Bible writer is just beating the drum for piety. Having no better arguments, he is trying to frighten us back to God by lurid pictures drawn out of his own imagination." That may be true, but do we have to take the *Psalmist's* word about the moral corruption and degradation of an atheistic society? Nazi-ism denied God and showed us what a short step it was from atheism to gas chambers. Communism, which is an avowedly anti-God way of life, recognizes no obligation save to itself; it has no respect for objective truth; it does everything from ulterior motives; it ridicules honesty and personal freedom; it treats human life as fodder, prostitutes it to slave labour, brainwashes it, murders it or simply starves it to death. Human nature has not changed greatly through the centuries. The practice of religion preserves for us our early instinct to be shocked at evil; its neglect kills that instinct. Let a man throw his religion overboard, let him lose the moral reference of Sinai and Galilee and trust his own standards for guidance, and he will presently find himself doing what once he would have shuddered at. We might do worse than adopt the Psalmist's attitude of declaring the godless, however powerful and successful, to be the subnormal, the morons of society.

You need not be especially pious to believe that religion plays an essential role in maintaining the stability and the decency of human society. The most worldly and sophisticated men – scientists, educators, engineers, surgeons, economists,

34

and statesmen—will agree with you entirely. If you enjoy going to a good circus, then you will know the name of P. T. Barnum. He was the greatest circus proprietor ever to travel the sawdust trails of the United States. He was also a religious man. When someone asked Barnum what he thought of the Church, he had this to say: "Show me a place where there are not any churches and where preachers are never seen, and I will show you a place where old hats are stuffed into windows, where the gates have no hinges, where the women are slipshod and where maps of the devil's wild land are printed on men's shirt bosoms in tobacco juice. That's what I will show you. Let us consider what the Church has done for us before we lightly esteem it."

As the converse of this truth, we see what happens to society when people turn back to God and there is a revival of true religion. Invariably it becomes linked with a revival of manners. In seventeenth-century England, when a decaying social structure swayed and tottered on the brink of a revolution as grim and ghastly as that taking place in France, one man, John Wesley, touched with evangelical fire the hearts of his fellow-countrymen, and out of that religious awakening came a passion for social reform that swept the length and breadth of this land like a prairie fire, so that historians writing of England's modern period divide it into two parts—before Wesley, and after Wesley. Must we not pray that the Holy Spirit of God will stir the hearts of people again, because there is surely no answer to the shocking deterioration in the morals of our society—the crimes, the violence, the sadism, the loose sexual behaviour—as long as churches remain empty and good people remain indifferent to religion. To be sure, *they* may seem to manage nicely without it, but what about their children and grandchildren? The history of many families is that the first generation is religious, the second learned, the third worldly, and the fourth has no history.

In yet another sense the Psalmist approaches our question, "Is Religion Necessary?" Do we need religion as a part of our psychological equipment? Does it make us more adequate to the demands of life? Does something essential go out of our lives when we exclude from them all the symbols and all the institutions that relate to spiritual realities, when we organize our lives on a materialistic basis? The obvious way to find an answer is to look at people who do try to get along without religion. We decided at the outset that many of them manage nicely, but that does not express the whole truth about them. The Psalmist brings his description of the godless society to a mounting crescendo, "There they were in great fear . . ." That is God's final judgment on people who ignore him: fear, tension, panic, expiring hopes.

Walter Lippmann has written that the greatest danger of the moment is the type of character that has been produced *en masse* in our time by those who have spent their jet-propelled lives trying to defy the God they did not like in Sunday School, and who seem successfully to have defied him, but who in the process have lost their nerve for living. Surely Lippmann has put his finger on a striking characteristic of our generation when he talks about people who have lost their nerve for living. Never have so many people exhibited signs of their inadequacy for the demands and the tensions of life. The suicide rate is higher today than it has ever been (five thousand in Britain last year); the number of chronic drinkers has risen in our society, people who have to drink in order to stiffen their backbone for quite mundane responsibilities; the consumption of aspirin and sleeping pills is altogether prodigious; we devour literature that gives us an emotional lift, films that provide an emotional escape; everywhere we are enlarging our mental hospitals, and we quite casually describe some of our friends as neurotics. Our generation will probably go down in history as a neurotic generation.

But that is understandable. Never has any generation lived in such fear of total destruction by forces which it seemed powerless to control. The Psalmist described us perfectly. "There they were in great fear . . ." Perhaps he saw or remembered a sudden dark storm cloud, evidence of the gathering wrath of God. "There," he cried—you can almost see his pointing finger; above, the storm cloud; and huddled beneath it, a crowd of worldlings with pallid faces and startled eyes—"there, in that bomb-proof shelter, that underground headquarters, there they are in great fear." This, according to the Psalmist, is the logical fruit of atheism. People get it into their heads that they do not need God, and so they become like ships that have broken loose from their moorings and are at the mercy of a furious ocean. Earth's foundations tremble, and the godless tremble too; they lose their nerve because they have lost their grip on the realities which are unshakable and abiding.

In his little book, *The Valley of the Shadow*, Bishop Hanns Lilje, one of the heroes of the German Resistance Movement during the war, describes his experiences in a Nazi concentration camp. Again and again he tells that what gave some prisoners greater courage than others to endure privation, indignity and torture was the fact that they clung so stubbornly to their religious faith. You could distinguish, he says, between the prisoners who possessed a living religion and those who lacked it. The first group were simply not afraid any more; they had conquered their fears, even the fear of death. Lilje himself tells that though his own execution appeared imminent, yet having contemplated death in the light of his Christian Faith, even the bars on his window and the chains on his wrists seemed no longer to have much meaning. He writes, "In those days it was granted me to tread the shores of that land which lies on the outermost fringe of time, upon which already something of the radiance of the other world is shining. I did not know that an existence which is still earthly and human could be so open to the world of God. It was a stillness full of blessing, a solitude over which God brooded, an imprisonment blessed by God himself."[1]

To such men as Bishop Lilje the question, "Is Religion Necessary?" has no reality. With them religion is not a fruit on a tree that may or may not be plucked; it is the very air that they breathe, the very atmosphere in which all things live and move and have their being. They do not argue about God; they live in God, they open their lives to God; and in the sense of his Presence their lives achieve strength and courage and meaning.

[1] Hanns Lilje, *The Valley of the Shadow* (The Muhlenberg Press, Philadelphia).

3

The Invisible God

SOME twelve years ago there was a radio debate between
Lord Bertrand Russell and a Jesuit priest, Father F. C.
Coppleston, on the subject, "The Existence of God". Paul
Edwards reproduces it verbatim in his collection of Bertrand
Russell's essays, published under the general title, *Why I Am
Not a Christian*.[1] Having defined God as "a supreme personal
being distinct from the world and creator of the world",
Father Coppleston proposed the thesis that such a being
actually exists and that his existence can be proved philo-
sophically. He then proceeded along three lines of argument,
the metaphysical, the moral, and the argument from religious
experience, and in each case Russell presented the opposite
view. "I am not contending," he said, "in a dogmatic way
that there is not a God. What I'm contending is that we
don't know that there is." Finally Coppleston asked him,
"Perhaps you would tell me whether your position is that of
agnosticism or atheism." Russell replied, "My position is
agnostic."

One can imagine that Lord Russell spoke those words
quite happily. Many people seem happy in their agnosticism.
They would never confess uncertainty in relation to other
things — their marriage, their business dealings or their choice
of a life's work — but when it comes to belief in the ultimate
Reality, they seem altogether proud and most anxious to
inform the whole world that they simply do not know.
Others treat their doubts more seriously. A young lady wrote
me a letter, then came for an interview to ask one question,
"How do we know that there is a God?", and you could see
at once that this was no academic question with her. It
touched the deepest issues of her life. She thirsted for assurance of God as an animal in the dry season thirsts for water.

This book attempts, however inadequately, to answer

[1] Bertrand Russell, *Why I Am Not a Christian* (George Allen and Unwin,
London, 1957).

some of the questions of honest doubt. I am convinced that many people, far from being content with agnosticism, recognize it as an important stage in their spiritual pilgrimage, but yearn to go beyond it to the firm ground of Christian assurance. For the present, however, certain obstacles of a practical and theoretical nature block their path, none more disturbing than the sheer difficulty of believing in a God whom they cannot see. Believe in love, yes; you can see your parents and children. Believe in democracy, yes; you need only visit the House of Commons. Believe in science, yes; its experiments can be proved. But the Gospel writer himself admits that "No one has ever seen God".

Someone has said that "the world is a kind of spiritual kindergarten where millions of bewildered infants are trying to spell G O D with the wrong blocks". God cannot be spelled in blocks of logic, because God is not a theorem to be worked out mathematically. God cannot be spelled in blocks of science, because God is not an object to be weighed and measured. God is a Person to be known, and we shall never know a person until we trust him and follow him and try to make him our friend. We believe in God, not because we have proved him; rather, we try to prove him because we believe in him. There is only one pathway to certainty and that lies through a venture of faith, "betting your life," as Donald Hankey said, "that there *is* a God."

Not irrational faith, however. To be sure, "no one has ever seen God", but neither had most Americans, before the advent of films and television, seen their President, nor most Englishmen seen their King. Yet no American and no Englishman in their right senses would have denied the existence of President and King. Too much in their common life gave evidence of administration and monarchy. If a man on the street says to you, "There is no Queen in Buckingham Palace, because I have never seen her," you will point him to all kinds of laws and institutions and customs and symbols in our British society, and ask him, "How do you explain these?" By the same token, while it may seem reasonable to disbelieve in a God whom we cannot see, yet the trouble with atheism or its milder and more polite cousin, agnosticism, is that they leave so much unexplained.

During the war, when the clouds were blackest and death rained from the skies, a brave clergyman in England

39

preached a sermon on the subject, "How Difficult Not To Believe in God". The preacher contended that while some men may have trouble convincing themselves about the reality of a God whom they cannot see, yet there are greater difficulties in the way of unbelief than there are in the way of belief. That will be our approach to the question, "How do we know that there is a God?" We shall not apologize for our faith. We shall not defend ourselves against the agnostic. Instead we shall put him on the defensive and we shall ask him: Since you are unwilling to believe in God because you cannot be sure, what have you accepted in God's place? There are certain phenomena which men of faith have always explained in terms of God's Creatorhood and Sovereignty and Love; how do *you* account for them?

I

For example, how do you explain the created universe? That was one of the major points in the debate between Lord Russell and the Jesuit priest. Contending that the existence of God can be proved by metaphysics, Father Coppleston advanced what philosophers call the "cosmological" argument; it means simply that nothing created itself; nothing contains within itself the reason for its own existence; everything, even the universe, must have a cause; and when you push back the evolutionary process to its beginning, you come to the uncreated Source of all creation, which is God. Russell, however, contended that the notion of the world having an explanation is a mistake. He said, "I see no reason to suppose that the total has any cause whatsoever." How would he explain the universe, then? He replied, "I would say that the universe is just there, and that's all."

But that is not all so far as the great philosophers or the men of simple faith are concerned. They believe that regardless of whether the universe came into being gradually or with a "big bang", the universe is not eternal and it did not create itself. Even those thinkers who cannot proceed beyond the threshold of theism to belief in a God who answers prayer and performs miracles, even these, when they contemplate the mystery, the immensity and the variety of creation are constrained to believe in a Creator. Nature to their eyes is like a painting that bears not only the signature but the character of the Artist. They know that man has made many wonderful things, great structures, intricate mechanisms and delicate instruments, but they look through a telescope at the Milky Way, they listen to the thunderous roar of Niagara, they catch their breaths at the sight of the Grand Canyon, they marvel at the glory of a sunset or the beauty of a desert flower or the awesomeness of an ocean storm, and they say with humility, "These things were created, and man did not create them."

We have not yet outgrown William Paley's classic illustration about the man crossing a field who strikes his foot against a stone which, for all he knows, may have been there forever. Further along he finds a watch, but he knows immediately that it has not been there forever. For when he examines it, he discovers that its parts have been framed and put together for a purpose, that they are so adjusted so as to produce motion, and the motion so regulated as to point to the hour of the day. Therefore, he concludes that the watch must have had an intelligent maker and designer. From this analogy Paley argued that everything in the natural world —the stars in their courses, the regularity of the seasons, the symmetry of the human body—suggest purpose and design. All support a modern translation of John's Gospel, "In the beginning was Mind, and the Mind was with God, and the Mind was God."

One of the most gracious and winsome personalities in Canadian higher education was the late Principal R. C. Wallace of Queens University in Kingston. Dr. Wallace was a geologist, a man who had spent a lifetime surveying the whole sweep of natural history through the geological ages and the process of evolution, and because he was a great scientist he possessed a winsome humility. His students would describe him as a Christly man. He may not have subscribed to the whole body of Christian orthodoxy, but he lived a life very close to God and he nurtured his faith in the fellowship of the Christian Church. In January 1955, during his last illness, Dr. Wallace addressed what might be called a final valedictory to his colleagues, students and friends. He wrote,

"As a scientist, I have not been able to convince myself that the marvellous articulation and adaptation both of living things and of inanimate nature can have come itself or through the

41

purely impersonal working of evolutionary laws alone. I feel that there is a mind beyond the visible processes, a fountainhead of all the love and beauty and goodness and truth which we as human beings so imperfectly reflect, a power that gives us freedom of choice, and an eternal hope. We call that power God. No one who truly loves nature can be satisfied that this life is all. For in the contemplation of the sunset or the storm, the minerals in the rock or the brilliance of the butterfly, the mind is caught up into a relationship that is beyond the world of passing things. We reach out into the eternal."

II

We ask the agnostic: if we have not sufficient evidence to believe in God, then how shall we explain the movement and purpose of history? Of course, many would reply that history has no movement, no purpose. They echo the poet who described history as "one damn thing after another", just a succession of unrelated facts. By themselves these facts may have meaning, but taken together they suggest no predetermined pattern, no continuous plot running through the whole story. Man makes his own history. In each generation he takes certain ingredients from the past and present, mixes them with his own genius or stupidity, and out comes history. That is one point of view.

The secular historian, Professor Charles A. Beard, advances another viewpoint. When someone asked him what major lessons he had learned from history, he answered that he had learned four: "First, whom the gods would destroy they make mad with power; second, the mills of God grind slowly, yet they grind exceeding small; third, the bee fertilizes the flower it robs; fourth, when it is dark enough, you see the stars." In that point of view history is the story of God with man and man with God. History is the sphere of God's activity. Having set history in motion, God accepts responsibility for it, presides over it, rules it and controls it according to his own purpose. History, if we study it closely enough, is like a window into the character of God; through it we can see God at work, the Master of all time, the supreme Genius who bestrides the centuries, keeping his hand on all passing events, shaping them, changing them according to his own designs. In this point of view history has no explanation apart from God.

The man who denies God will have trouble explaining certain events in history—Creation itself, for example. Macneille Dixon has said somewhere that had he been present at the birth of this planet, and had some archangel turned to tell him that this blazing mass, this whirlpool of unbelievable fire with its heat of roughly fifty million degrees, was on its way to cool and become the cradle of civilization and culture, he would have determined never to talk with such a demented, deranged angel again. The emergence of a single nation, Israel, to become the greatest spiritual community the world has ever known, and its stubborn survival through seventeen centuries of slavery, exile, oppression and dispersion, defies explanation. So does the birth of Christianity—history bisected, its whole course changed by the followers of a man murdered on a cross. In the language of faith we speak of these things as Creation, Providence and Redemption, God's mighty acts in history. Without God, what shall we call them?

The man who denies God will have trouble explaining the *development* of certain events in history. The agnostic attributes all events to human causes, but can you name a single human cause why Christianity should have survived through the first three centuries of the Christian era? Everything added up to its early extinction. By every human calculation Jesus should have become just another innocuous god in the Roman pantheon. The historian, if he were a man of faith, could single out the specific instances in history where two plus two have equalled five; he could say to us, "Lo, here! Lo, there! God was at work, administering justice, breaking down evil and building up good." He might even hesitate to use the name of God; he might speak of an inner dynamism in history or a moral purpose, but he would leave no doubt that, whatever we call it, there is running through history a Power, not our own, that makes for righteousness.

III

We ask the agnostic yet another question: If we cannot believe in God, how shall we explain personal religious experience? One thing that always puzzles me about a man like Bertrand Russell is the fact that his solitariness never

43

seems to bother him. He stands quite apart from the majority of men in every culture and generation. The most primitive and the most civilized men have believed in God, by whatever name they called him—Tien, Ahura-Mazda, Amon, Allah, Jehovah, Father. Dr. Dale of Birmingham once wrote by way of comparison, "If I were the only person who saw the sun rise this morning, then I might doubt my experience and call myself the victim of an illusion. But if I hear that many people in different countries and of varied intellectual powers have seen the same thing; and if I am told that men and women have laid down their lives rather than deny its reality, then my doubt vanishes and I become sure of myself."

It is possible, of course, that mankind may from the dawn of consciousness have been deluded by its universal religious experience. H. L. Mencken once declared that belief in God issues from "the puerile egos of inferior men". Referring to this statement, an American preacher, John Haynes Holmes, listed a few of the so-called "inferior men"—Socrates, Plato, Cicero, Seneca, Descartes, Spinoza, Kant, Goethe, Gandhi, Fiske, Eddington, Lodge and numerous others. There have been great agnostics, of course, profound thinkers who probed the mystery of existence and could not honestly get beyond a humanistic and materialistic explanation, and for their honest doubt we must respect them. The garden variety, however, had better examine their own motives and decide whether their unbelief does not grow out of emotional disappointment, moral laziness or the reluctance to be committed. After all, what is easier and cheaper and less involved in life than to say, "I don't know."

Conducting a mission at McGill University, Canon C. R. Raven told the students that for years he has treasured what he calls his picture gallery—the memory of the long series of incidents and events in which the awareness of God has blazed suddenly and vividly upon him. They are a curious and miscellaneous collection and they run to strange places, some of them rather terrible places: bits of France in the First World War; dead people; young lovers in back streets; a crowd of squalid, shawl-clad women getting fish and chips from a greasy fellow dispensing them under a naphtha flare in a Liverpool slum. But "suddenly the glory!" Canon Raven went on to tell these young undergraduates, "Test

44

your own picture gallery and see if you don't get an enlarged sensitiveness from recalling those moments in which the opaque world became transparent and you saw through into the truer life of the eternal."[1]

In the last analysis, that is the only answer we can give to the young lady who asked, "How do we know that there is a God?" You will never find God by reaching up to heaven and searching for him. If you really long for God, you will be found by him in experiences through which eternity penetrates time like sunlight breaking through the clouds. Such experiences may be rare but they are real; and the fact that you cannot impart or even describe them to other people is no proof that they have not happened. The atheist may tell you as he told Bunyan's Pilgrim, "There is no Celestial City!", but you have one reply, and whether it satisfies him or not, it satisfies you, "I saw the Celestial City from the top of Mount Clear!"

IV

One final question to the agnostic: If there is no God, how shall we account for the Christian Faith? Whenever doubt casts its shadow upon our convictions, the best way of judging them is resolutely to examine their alternatives. Suppose for the moment we agree with the brilliant Bertrand Russell that while there may be a God, yet we really do not know because we have not sufficient evidence to prove his existence. In the meantime we have no alternative but to reshape our thinking and reorganize our lives on the supposition that there is not a God. It means that we have been a part of the most colossal hoax ever perpetrated on the human race over nineteen centuries. It means that all the churches, all the cathedrals, every building erected in the name of Christ have been founded on a monstrous lie. The saints are psychopaths, the martyrs neurotics, and a man like Albert Schweitzer a sentimental fool.

An agnostic position, consistently followed, reduces to the category of myth, legend and fiction that remarkable library of books which we call the Bible. Can we name any other collection of writings, gathered together over a period of a thousand years, all dealing with a subject which has been

[1] C. R. Raven, *Christ and the Modern Opportunity* (Ryerson Press).

exploded as untrue? The Bible from cover to cover is predicated on one truth, namely, that man does know God, not only knows that God exists, but what God is like. The Bible takes God for granted; it no more tries to prove his existence than a biography of Napoleon tries to prove the existence of Napoleon. The Bible writers are not philosophers; they are more like newspaper reporters giving us their account of something which has happened to them. They have looked upon the wonders of nature and seen there the signature of God; they have looked back over their nation's history and discerned a power, not their own, working for righteousness; they have looked into their own lives and recalled experiences of help and comfort and chastening and guidance from beyond. Scripture has no meaning for the man who refuses to believe in God.

What will such a man do with Jesus Christ? Russell, of course, makes the outlandish claim that "historically it is quite doubtful whether Christ ever existed at all", and he certainly questions both the wisdom and the moral integrity of the man portrayed in the Gospels. But why stop there? If we do not know that there is a God, then Jesus was not only unwise and immoral; he was history's most deluded and insane character. He deserved to be crucified, because he spoke of God in as intimate terms as a man speaks of his father. And his followers deserved to be martyred, because they not only accepted what Jesus told them about God; they believed that God lived in Jesus in a very special way. There seemed no other explanation to this altogether unique person, so perfect in character and magnetic in leadership, who taught people with such authority, who forgave sins, healed the sick and raised the dead and by his presence and words made God the most real fact in their experience.

A great German once drew a terrible imaginative picture of Jesus returning to earth and confessing with shame that all his teaching about God was a mistake; that he had gone beyond into the great Unknown and found there no Father God behind things after all, but instead an awful cosmic nothingness. How should we react to so ghastly a revelation? With sorrow, despair, panic? Or would we simply look at Jesus, this winsome, sinless Man of Galilee, and say to him, "It doesn't matter. Your life is still the best I know. I cannot call the best I know a lie. I must call the best I know the

46

truth. As long as *you* remain in this universe, I shall desire no other God beside you." That, perhaps, is how we ought to react—our final answer to the question, "How do we know that there is a God?" "No one has ever seen God," declares the Gospel writer. But, he adds triumphantly, "the only Son, who is in the bosom of the Father, he has made him known."

4

The Impact of Science

Is THERE any room for religious faith in the modern
world of science? In attempting to answer that question,
this chapter is addressed specifically to three people.

First, a minister of the Gospel, an evangelical of the
fundamentalist type. He preaches to large congregations
made up of people who agree with him, and he preaches
with the most naïve disregard of modern theological scholar-
ship. I heard him give a sermon on the Old Testament book
of *Daniel* and I thought afterward, "This could have been
given a hundred years ago. It pays no attention to the whole
movement of Biblical criticism; indeed it takes no account
of any change in the human situation over the past century."
The preacher did make one slight reference to science and
its impact on religion, but only to say that we have nothing
to fear from it. He said that scientists are always changing
their minds and contradicting their own theories. Any
scientific textbook has to be rewritten after five years, but
God's Word is eternally relevant. The Gospel is everlasting.
Like a great mountain it has survived all the storms of the
centuries and it will survive the storm of science.

Second, a young scientist, though even he might not call
himself such. Let us say that he holds a Ph.D. degree and
earns his living by working at science. I met him for the first
time when he came with his fiancée to discuss plans for their
wedding. She was a lovely girl who came from a fine church
family, a girl who herself had been very close to the Church
and to whom the Christian Faith had deep meaning. I coun-
selled this excellent young man that though he might have
no room in his thinking for a spiritual interpretation of life,
yet he must not take away from his bride that which she
counted infinitely precious. He listened patiently and said
nothing. The fact is, however, that much to the sorrow of her
parents she has now drifted away from the Church entirely;
you can't go on fighting a losing battle in your own home.

48

Sometimes the parents suggest tactfully to their daughter and her husband that they should have the baby baptized, but the young scientist is too honest for that. He simply smiles and asks, "Why?"

Third, a medical student, also the product of a Christian home, and himself a youth of great idealism. He wavered for a time between medicine and the ministry and chose medicine because he believed that God wanted him to be a doctor. After about two years at university he came to see me in a disturbed frame of mind, and you could tell that he had been given the full treatment—books, lectures, experiments, agnostic professors, discussions late into the night. He had no sophomoric arrogance. He just said, "I am not sure what I can believe any more." His difficulty was threefold. First, he had been thoroughly schooled in the scientific method which insists that every hypothesis shall be tested and proved before it can be believed, and religion did not seem to fit into this category. Second, it had been pointed out to him that the Bible and the historic Christian Creeds came out of a prescientific age which was ignorant of evolution and which presupposed a universe with the earth at its centre. Third, he saw that as the various sciences pushed back the frontiers of knowledge and cleared up areas of mystery, there seemed no place left in the scheme of things for the supernatural, and he wondered if God might not eventually be put out of a job, crowded out of the picture altogether. Science had made its full impact on him. On the one hand, he did not want to lose his childhood faith; yet on the other hand, he wanted to be loyal to this new discipline. But could the two be reconciled? Is there any room for religious faith in the modern world of science?

I

Addressing these three people, I turn first to the minister of the Gospel, and, as gently as possible, I tell him to stop making a fool of himself. The story of the conflict between science and religion is not a happy one, and the Church has sometimes aggravated it by clinging to the past and stubbornly refusing to accept the implications of new truth. In popular imagination the conflict was seriously joined exactly one hundred years ago at Oxford when Thomas Huxley and

Bishop Wilberforce publicly debated Darwin's *Origin of Species*. The Bishop made a polished and witty but superficial speech, ending with an objectionable allusion to human descent from an ape. He asked "if anyone were willing to trace his descent through an ape as his grandfather, would he be willing to trace his descent similarly on the side of his grandmother", hoping by his misplaced humour to arouse a sentimental objection to the idea of woman being so degraded. Huxley, murmuring to his neighbour, "The Lord hath delivered him into my hands" (strange comment for an agnostic!), gave a plain and honest account of Darwin's scientific views and ended to the effect that he would rather have a monkey for his grandfather than one who used great gifts to stifle truth.

The Church appears just a little ridiculous when it preaches the Gospel as though nothing had happened to challenge that Gospel over the past hundred years, and more especially when it rates modern science as just another storm that the Gospel will eventually weather. Christianity has never encountered anything comparable to the impact of modern science. Professor Herbert Butterfield says that the scientific revolution of the sixteenth and seventeenth centuries "outshines anything since the rise of Christianity and reduces the Renaissance and the Reformation to the rank of mere episodes, mere internal displacements within the system of medieval Christendom". The Church today lives in a totally new situation. The one supreme fact with which it must reckon is the advent of a new way of thinking and a new way of living brought to pass through the discoveries of science. If the Church fails here, then it becomes as irrelevant as some of its critics would make it out to be.

There is a homely story about a farmer in the Southern United States who took a pair of fighting cocks to an illegal gaming establishment where they were scheduled to do battle with another pair. He transported them in the back of his truck but made the mistake of putting them in the same cage. When he arrived, the two birds were exhausted and bleeding because they had been fighting each other along the way. Disgustedly the man exclaimed, "Didn't someone tell those fool roosters they were on the same side?"

Surely it needs someone to tell the more dogmatic men of science and the more dogmatic men of religion that they are on the same side. To be sure, science becomes a rival when men worship it in such a way as to rule out other necessary and legitimate devotions such as those implicit in the Christian Faith. The Church, however, has abundant reason to thank God for science, and not only for its material benefits which make possible the extension of Christ's ministry to the ends of the earth, but also for the change that science has wrought in people's thinking, releasing them from superstition, ignorance and fatalism, and schooling them in the concept of an orderly, law-abiding universe.

Not for a moment do I presume to pass personal judgment on my brother minister. As a man of God and a curer of souls he may be endowed with Divine grace and power. As an interpreter of Christian truth, however, he represents that perennial tendency of the Church to fight a rearguard action instead of coming to head-on terms with a situation that challenges orthodoxy. The new world view brought into being by the discoveries of science does constitute a barrier to belief for a great many people, but we shall not break down that barrier by walking around it and shouting like the Israelites as they encircled the walls of Jericho. As Christians we must quietly rethink our position, never afraid of discarding old truth or of embracing new truth, but always probing more deeply into the eternal truths and seeking to express them in the thought-forms of our own day. This is not a human exercise. God himself, by the promised power of his Holy Spirit, will lead us to new adventures in Christian understanding, *if* we have the courage to follow his initiatives.

II

Next, we address ourselves to the young scientist. We shall not argue with him, because argument only hardens people in their prejudices and because the object of Christian apologetics is not to win arguments but to win men. Besides, he will quickly remind me that I really have no competence to discuss scientific questions, and he will be right. The fact that a man may be partially-qualified as a theologian does not entitle him to speak authoritatively in other fields. But that surely applies to the scientist as well who, though he may be an expert in biochemistry, is not necessarily an expert in the humanities or even in some other branch of science. Certainly his scientific training does not make him an expert in the knowledge of the Bible and theology. When the mathematician speaks on mathematics he deserves to be heard; when he speaks on religion, his opinion may be no better than that of any other layman.

We shall tell our friend also that the scientific method of observation, experiment, induction and generalization does not apply to the whole of reality. Life is the business of the poet as well as the physiologist, the artist as well as the astronomer. Every phenomenon may have a scientific explanation, but science does not exhaust the explanation. Is it enough, for example, to describe the excitement of two lovers in terms of an accelerated release of adrenalin into the blood; or a mother caring for her child as the preservation of the race; or the mind of Shakespeare as an intricate network of nerve endings; or an exquisite violin solo as a musician scraping the hair of one animal over the entrails of another? Man lives in at least two worlds: one of science in which questions posed in scientific terms allow of scientific answers; and a world of love and beauty and truth and goodness and sorrow and faith that defies the worker in the laboratory.

Science, after all, does have limitations, and scientists themselves are sometimes the first to acknowledge it. We have seen in our own generation what science can do, but we have also seen what it cannot do. We know that science can modernize a house, but it can never turn a house into a home. Science can make penicillin for the healing of the body but it cannot minister to a guilty conscience or pluck from the memory a rooted sorrow. Science can split the atom, but it cannot resolve the problems that nuclear fission creates. Science can put terrifying powers into the hands of man, but not necessarily the moral strength to use those powers wisely. There is sharp point in the Persian legend of the three scientists crossing the desert. The first one pronounced his magic formula, and immediately the dust of the desert framed the skeleton of a lion. The second conjured up his magic word, and immediately the skeleton was clothed with hide and hair. The third pronounced his incantation, and life suddenly came into the lion. Whereupon the beast rose and gobbled up all three scientists.

Much of the hostility between science and religion flows from the utterly false assumption that each must be controlled by a different spirit. People think that we reach scientific truth along the avenue of pure reason, and religious truth along the avenue of pure faith. On the one hand, you believe what can be seen and proved; on the other hand, you are supposed to believe what cannot be seen and proved. This point of view does gross injustice to both religion and science and is certainly not a true picture of life as we experience it. All of life in all its relationships is a blending of reason and faith, and nowhere is this more true than in a scientific laboratory. Look at the great scientist as he enters his laboratory to begin research. He comes in honesty, integrity and hope. He has a humility before the created order of things which are to be received and studied. He brings a sense of high dedication, a passion for his work, without regard to its material rewards. He brings faith in its highest sense, which is the willingness to stake everything on his hypotheses, to expend years of patient, sacrificial labour, hoping for success, yet willing to fail if it helps others to build constructively on the foundation of his mistakes. Is that so foreign to the spirit of true religion?

A moment ago we reminded ourselves of the debt that religion owes to science. It were well to remind our young friend that science in its turn owes a debt to religion. We cannot argue, perhaps, as some have done, that science is a fruit of Christianity, but we can certainly recall that science grew up within a Christian tradition and that the early scientists were men of deep religious convictions, some of them in Holy Orders. Kepler pursued his theories because he believed that a perfect God made the universe perfectly. Paracelsus was led to his discovery of the use of minerals in medicine by his conviction that God had provided remedies in nature for the various diseases. Isaac Newton declared that his theological studies were as important as his strictly scientific ones. The Somerset Friar Roger Bacon wrote a paper to the effect that the new scientific knowledge, far from being an enemy of the Christian Faith, was actually an aid, even in the business of evangelizing mankind. It is no accident that the scientific revolution, which could only have been possible within a climate of free inquiry, should have taken place in the centuries since the Protestant Reformation. In the early years science and religion walked together as handmaidens of the same objective truth. At one time

53

religion, morals, science and aesthetics all owned a common discipline. Now knowledge has become atomized, science become a narrower discipline, and many scientists themselves are strangers to large areas of reality.

One final word to this young man who has taken away his wife's religious faith rather than attempt to share it with her. If a scientific education must inevitably lead to agnosticism, then why are all the great scientists not unbelievers? Albert Einstein, though he belonged to no orthodox religious community, described himself as a profoundly religious man. When someone asked Sir James Simpson, who discovered the use of chloroform as an anaesthetic, to name the greatest discovery he had ever made, Simpson replied, "The greatest discovery I ever made was that I was a great sinner and Jesus Christ a wonderful Saviour." Recently I read two articles by Wernher von Braun, the world's leading expert on guided-missile development. In one of them he gives a scientific preview of man's first flight to the moon; in the other he tells of his own spiritual experiences as a man of prayer. These men are great scientists, but they know that science is only a partial response to part of our environment. Religion is man's total response to his total environment, and in that response he achieves his greatness as a man.

III

Now we turn to the young medical undergraduate. In confessing, "I am not sure what I can believe any more," he represents a great many people who find themselves torn between traditional beliefs and the new world view effected by the discoveries of modern science. The conflict, though it may now be less dramatic on the public stage, remains unresolved in their own minds, and they are not satisfied to resolve it by moving exclusively in one direction or the other. On the one hand, they accept the disciplines and the implications of scientific truth; on the other hand, they are prepared to rethink their Christian Faith if someone will guide them in a way that respects their intelligence. Is there a Word of God that will give them light and reassurance in the darkness of their confused thinking? I believe that there is, and that it is bound up with all that we know about the great Biblical doctrines of the Christian Faith.

First, *the doctrine of Creation.* This doctrine is basic to all other Christian beliefs. It proclaims the truth that the universe and everything in it is the product of a Creative Mind; that the solar system, the stars, the galaxies, the oceans, the mountains, the forests, the minerals, the living organisms owe their existence to a creative act of God. This doctrine concerns itself not with the techniques but with the fact of Creation. It stands over against the theory that things merely emanated from nothing or that the world owes its existence to a force other than God. If this doctrine be true, then it means that scientific discoveries no less than moral and spiritual discoveries are the revelation of God. It means that all truth is Divine truth and, therefore, has the quality of givenness about it. Man discovers truth, but he does not create it; man probes the secrets of nature, but they are still the secrets of nature; he works the works of God, but they are still the works of God. Man does not add anything to the scheme of things; he takes what God gives him and manipulates it either for his own well-being or his own destruction. In this point of view science does not crowd God out of the universe; rather it opens up new possibilities of understanding the nature of God's universe and the nature of him who made it.

Second, *the doctrine of Providence*, which means that God who created this universe has not withdrawn to a distant heaven and allowed the universe to run itself. You remember that deluge of questions that came pouring out of the whirlwind at the unhappy Job — not easy questions; the wisest scientist would have difficulty answering them today. "Where were you when I laid the foundation of the earth? Tell me, if you have understanding!" And God continues: What holds up the world? Why does the law of gravity keep the earth in its orbit? Who decided how big the world should be? Who determines where the sea shall stop and the land begin? Can you make the morning come when you are ready? Do you cause the day to end and the night to draw near? Do you know how the sun makes its light? Can you make the thunder or lightning or cause the wind to blow in any direction you desire? Can you bring dew to the earth or frost? Can you change the stars in the sky or rearrange the constellations? Do you understand how the wild animals in the wilderness regulate their lives? God is telling Job that this is an orderly world that we inhabit, a dependable, kindly world. How can we escape the conviction that behind it is a caring Providence who keeps all things under his sovereign control? God is not less wonderful but more wonderful and more worthy of our worship when we cease looking for him in the world of supernature and begin looking for him in the world of nature where he can really be found.

Third, *the doctrine of Redemption*, which means that by dwelling for a season in One who was bone of our bone and flesh of our flesh, God has brought together in perfect unity the material and spiritual worlds. In Jesus Christ God has broken down the dividing wall between sacred and secular and shown himself involved in our temporal as well as our eternal destiny. In giving his Son to die upon the Cross God has laid claim to material things; he has purchased them —science as well as religion, the laboratory as well as the sanctuary, the research worker as well as the priest. In raising Christ from the dead God has proclaimed his sovereignty over the whole of life and has opened for us a new and living way by which the work of our hands shall be redeemed from selfish and destructive use and turned to his own glory and the good of all mankind.

Is there any room for religious faith in the modern world of science? There are many books that will answer that question affirmatively, none more searching and readable than *Science and Christian Belief* by C. A. Coulson, the Professor of Applied Mathematics at Oxford University. Dr. Coulson believes that, far from outdating and nullifying traditional Christian beliefs, science is playing an important part in the unfolding of the nature and purpose of God. He denies the dichotomy of faith and reason; he denies the division of life into material and spiritual. "There is no 'God of the gaps'," he says, "to take over at those places where science fails . . . Either God is in the whole of nature, with no gaps, or he is not there at all." "We have done wrong," he says, "to set up any sharp antithesis between science and religion. Science itself must be a religious activity . . . Science is one aspect of God's presence, and scientists, therefore, part of the company of his heralds."[1]

I want to introduce all three of my friends to one of God's heralds—the Chairman of the Physics Department in

[1] C. A. Coulson, *Science and Christian Belief*.

a great European University. He identified himself with my church during his brief period at the National Research Council in Ottawa some years ago. He is a scientist and a distinguished one, but first a committed Christian. As we chatted together he said, in effect, "I wonder sometimes if I ought to remain in this work. I want more than anything to serve Jesus Christ, and it may be that I could serve him better by leaving the field of science and entering some humanitarian sphere." We often talked this way, but before leaving Canada he said, "I think Christ really wants me to serve him as a scientist. I move among men who hold the world's immediate future in their hands and to whom great numbers of people look as the world's saviours. They respect me because I am one of them and because I have achieved some stature in my profession. My witness must be to them and to my students." And then he said, with feeling, "Perhaps even more than strong churches, the world today needs classrooms and scientific laboratories that recognize the Lordship of Jesus Christ."

5

The Space Age

ON APRIL 12th, 1961, a new age dawned in the history of mankind. On that day, between the hours we crawled out of bed and reached the office, a man-made rocket the size of a bus, carrying a young Russian, Major Yuri Gagarin, left its launching-pad, soared one hundred and eighty-five miles into outer space, circled the planet earth, and returned safely to its prearranged destination. Subsequently the Russians sent up another cosmonaut who circled the earth nineteen times; and these colossal achievements they have hailed as but the promise of greater victories to come.

Needless to say, the Soviets have not ignored the propaganda value of space-travel in their unceasing polemic against religion. Earlier this year the local Stanislav radio station commented:

"Every scientific achievement deals a crushing blow to the idea of the existence of God. The higher the altitude reached by the Soviet intellect, the less room there is for religion in the consciousness of the people. The date of April 12th, 1961 and the name of the cosmonaut, Yuri Gagarin, have been inscribed in history. Religion was dealt a mortal blow by the human intellect and by the builders of Communism."

Khruschev took a similar line by commenting ironically that Titov had seen no signs of God during his flight in space.

"No signs of God"—that describes our religious problem in the space age. We feel like a certain tadpole, if a tadpole does have feelings, which some children reared from an egg in a rose-bowl full of water. Each day they watched this tiny creature darting across his little globe, presumably happy in it and content with the food that was dropped to him. When he grew larger and developed legs and began taking on the appearance of a frog, he kept rising to the surface and struggling as if he wanted to escape. So one day

58

in solemn ceremony the children took the baby frog to a park and dropped him among the lily-pads at the edge of a lake. Can we imagine his brain, if such there be, reeling under the discovery that his little world was only a part of a much vaster creation and his tiny bowl of water as nothing compared to the millions of gallons of water in the lake? Can we imagine the tiny creature trying to feel at home in this expanded universe, trying to revise his thoughts about God? A God who made a rose-bowl he could understand, but a God who made a lake and lily-pads and trees and a park and other creatures is beyond his utmost stretch of thought. At first his feelings are so bewildered that he can see no signs of God at all.

Scientifically the Bible and the historic creeds are out of date. They presuppose a picture of the universe as it *appears* to us: a two-storey building with the earth on the main floor, heaven upstairs and hell down in the cellar. To the older theologians only earth mattered in the universe; all else existed for the sake of the earth, and man was the supreme object of earth's existence. Now the whole framework of this picture has been shattered, and so, we fear, has the picture itself. Every major Christian doctrine has to be re-thought in the light of the new scientific view of the universe. Did the universe have a beginning in time or did it exist eternally, and, if so, how does that affect our basic Christian belief in God as the Creator? Granted that there may be a creative Spirit behind and within the universe, is it really conceivable that in the midst of all this vastness he should be especially concerned with a microscopic speck of dust called "the earth"? We could believe in a God who contrived our small world with such ingenuity, but now, like the lowly tadpole, we move among other worlds, billions of them, and we wonder how our faith can stand up to the discovery.

In wrestling with this obstacle to Christian belief it is best to begin by recognizing that the new discoveries of science and space-travel are really not relevant to our faith. Controversies between learned men about the precise origin of the universe may fascinate us, but in the last analysis they make no difference to religion, and the more eminent scientists are the first to recognize it. Sir Bernard Lovell began his Reith Lectures on "The Individual and the Universe" by saying, "It is with mixed feelings of fear and humility that I start on the task of talking to you about the universe," and having acknowledged the limitations of science, he ended by saying, "I have lived my days as a scientist, but science has never claimed the whole of my existence." Such men know that though their discoveries may terrify or enthral us, they do not answer our ultimate questions; they know that it is not the business of science to find God, or not find him, in stellar space. God is not visible through a telescope, or from a space rocket. Titov saw no signs of God as he circled the earth nineteen times, but Titov, with his atheistic mind, is not competent to discern God. God is inaccessible to Titov.

The effect which the space age will have on our religious beliefs depends entirely upon where we stand. If we stand secure in the faith, the new scientific view of the universe will increase our faith; if we stand in scepticism, the new discoveries will increase our scepticism. To be sure, it comes as a shock when first we grasp the unimaginable vastness and variety of the universe, and we may well have to revise our ideas of God. The revision need not lead to atheism, however, but towards a larger and grander and more magnificent idea of God than we have ever dreamed. There was an old preacher in New England who every year preached a sermon to his rural congregation on the latest discoveries in astronomy. When somebody asked him what use such a sermon could have in such a place, he replied, "Why, none at all, but it greatly enlarges my idea of God." Let us compare Mr. Titov's experience with that of a young airman who was killed at the age of nineteen while serving with the Royal Canadian Air Force. Flying at an altitude of thirty thousand feet above England, John Gillespie Magee wrote these lines:

> "Oh! I have slipped the surly bonds of earth
>   And danced the skies on laughter-silvered wings;
> Sunward I've climbed, and joined the tumbling mirth
>   Of sun-split clouds—and done a hundred things
> You have not dreamed of—wheeled and soared and swung
>   High in the sunlit silence. Hov'ring there,
> I've chased the shouting wind along, and flung
>   My eager craft through footless halls of air.

Up, up the long, delirious, burning blue
   I've topped the wind-swept heights with easy grace
Where never lark, or even eagle flew—
And, while with silent lifting mind I've trod
   The high untrespassed sanctity of space,
Put out my hand and touched the face of God."[1]

In exactly that way the Bible approaches the problem of God in the Space Age, and let us not suppose that it was unknown to the Bible writers. Five centuries before Christ a Hebrew poet stood on the Judean hills and reflected on the mystery and variety of the universe, the moon and the stars and the glittering galaxies in heaven above, and its effect was not to shatter his religious faith but to confirm and strengthen it,

"When I consider thy heavens, the work of thy fingers, the moon and the stars, which thou hast ordained; What is man, that thou art mindful of him. . . ?"

Impressed as he was with the immensity of the universe, he was more impressed with the thought of God who created it, and still more with the interest of this cosmic God in his human creatures. Quoting the Psalmist and taking up the same theme in the New Testament, the writer of the Epistle to the Hebrews says in effect that we are not concerned with God in his relation to space, but in his relation to life. We do not know the God of the solar systems; *that* God is inaccessible to us. We only know the God who has revealed himself in Jesus Christ. Therefore we shall confine ourselves to our knowledge of God in Christ and in that knowledge we shall find wisdom to overcome other difficulties. "As it is, we do not yet see everything in subjection to him (i.e. to man), But we see Jesus . . ."

We look at Jesus, and we see *a human personality*. That is surely significant as we attempt to regain a sense of proportion in a universe that bulldozes us by its immensity. William Beebe, the naturalist, tells of a ritual through which he and the late President Theodore Roosevelt used to go. After an evening chat they would step outside and look up at the heavens. Searching with or without the aid of glasses until

---

[1] *Masterpieces of Religious Verse*, ed. by James Dalton Morrison, no. 225 (Harper and Brothers, New York, 1948).

they found the faint spot of light-mist beyond the lower left-hand corner of the great square of Pegasus, one of them would recite: "That is the Spiral Galaxy of Andromeda. It is as large as our Milky Way. It is one of a hundred million galaxies. It is seven hundred and fifty thousand light years away. It consists of one hundred billion suns, each larger than our sun." After an interval Roosevelt would grin and say, "Now, I think we are small enough! Let's go to bed."[1]

But who measures the importance of things by their size? Even in our human value-scales we do not rate bigness as the criterion of significance. We know that many of the most precious, most vital, most powerful things in life have to be observed through a microscope. We also know that nothing matters more than personality. Here is a man of great wealth, a captain of industry whose business enterprises reach all over the world and who can make and un-make policies and politicians with a stroke of his pen. Are these of first importance to him, if he is a father of children? No. He would exchange all of his great wealth, leave all his vast enterprises to run themselves, renounce all of his power in order to look to the welfare of his smallest child.

The Bible asks us to believe exactly that about God, and that is why the Bible tells us to keep our eyes focused on Jesus and our minds focused upon his teaching. He said, "Are not two sparrows sold for a penny? And not one of them will fall to the ground without your Father's will. But even the hairs of your head are all numbered." We shall never understand the immensities of outer space, but we can understand a human personality, and that is where we must look to find God. We must realize that personality is still the zenith of God's creation, still the crown and flower of the evolutionary process; that however wonderful the stars, they can never be so wonderful as the human eye that beholds them and the human brain that measures them. Astronomically speaking, man is not a grain of sand; he is the astronomer. He is not a speck of dust in space, but the space-traveller. The Psalmist realized that truth. What staggered him was not the planets and solar systems, but that God who brought the worlds into being should do for him what he does not do for all the planets and solar systems. He

[1] As related in *Communion Through Preaching* by Henry Sloane Coffin, pp. 16–17 (Charles Scribner's Sons, New York and London, 1952).

is mindful of him and visits him. He loves him with an ever-lasting love. In God's scale of values size is not of first importance, and though dwarfed by the cosmic universe, man is still in a spiritual sense the centre of the cosmic universe. Let the astronomers gaze through their telescopes and let the cosmonauts cruise through outer space; they will make many discoveries, but they will not find a higher and more marvellous creation than the human soul. Wrote Tennyson,

> "For though the giant ages heave the hill,
>   And break the shore,
>   And evermore
> Make and break and work their will;
>
> Though world on world in myriad myriads roll
>   Round us, each with different powers,
>   And other forms of life than ours,
> What know we greater than the soul?"

We look at Jesus, and we see *an act of redemption*. We see the Almighty and Eternal God, never visible among the stars and planets, making himself visible in a human personality and acting for our salvation. In his book, *World Without End*,[1] Roger Pilkington tells that some time ago when there was a press rumour that a flying saucer full of scaly little men had landed on our planet, he was talking with the dean of a cathedral. The dean said, "Do you realize that at any moment such a vehicle might land right here in the Deanery Yard? And if so," he added, "it would be my job as an ordained priest and minister of the Gospel to go out there and talk to the crew about the risen Christ. I confess that I find myself singularly ill-equipped for the task." Ill-equipped or not, the dean had caught the New Testament interpretation of God's act of redemption in Christ, an act performed not only for this world and this race, but for all worlds, all times and all souls.

Of course, that sounds like another example of man's colossal conceit, a product of the pre-scientific age when we believed that this planet was, in fact, the centre of the universe and the only locality inhabited by living creatures. Before rejecting that view, however, we ought to consider the fact that there is still reasonable doubt that living

[1] Collins Fontana Books.

creatures could exist on other planets. Having regard to the earth's temperature, its atmospheric pressure and its speed of rotation, it still seems to many scientists the only habitation in this vast stellar universe capable of producing, developing and supporting animate forms. Of all the other planets Mars and Venus alone approximate the geological conditions of earth, and the most reputable scientists are agreed that the odds are a thousand to one against either of them having all the conditions right for the existence of life. The centrality of our planet earth derives not from its physical size and position but from the fact that it is still the scene of God's greatest experiment, the experiment of personality; it is the nursery of the moral, intellectual and spiritual life of the whole universe, the one environment which has produced a self-conscious creature made in the image of God and capable of thinking God's thoughts after him.

How very naïve we are to suppose that the space age will be an embarrassment to the Bible! It only indicates that we have not fully understood the Bible writers, else we should realize that in their concept of God and their concept of the saving work of Christ they had a view of the universe that we are only now beginning to approximate. "God so loved the world that he gave his only begotten Son . . ." In this context the original Greek word for "world" is "cosmos", and it means the whole created universe, not just the countries that surrounded the Mediterranean Sea, not even the unexplored continents and oceans beyond, but the sun and the moon and the stars in the night sky and the galaxies so far away that their light takes centuries to reach us. As the New Testament writers saw it, the destiny of the entire universe is bound up with a race of creatures on this single planet. When man falls, he drags the world of nature down with him, and when this world falls it must be redeemed, because there are no other worlds, no other denizens of eternity or potential sons of God to take its place. God loses everything when he loses his human family. On this earth, therefore, God acted to redeem his human family. He came to this world, not to some distant galaxy; and he came not in a cosmic explosion but as a baby in a barn. Travel where we may through the universe, it is here we determine the destiny of the universe, here that the ultimate decision must be made.

We look at Jesus, and we see *a responsibility*. The most sobering word that can be spoken to us in this new age of astronomy and space-travel is that we should not lose our sense of proportion. Epoch-making as it may be, the new scientific view of the universe has not changed our essential situation or solved a single human problem. As one wise person said after the Russian cosmonauts had returned to earth with all their valuable scientific information,

"Nothing has been found up there that has changed the ground rules down here. Nothing has been gleaned along the Milky Way which has made the good life easier or the wrong less attractive. There is nothing out there that can warm one heart chilled with loneliness here, or bandage one mind that's bleeding to death from doubt, or forgive one sin that has turned one soul prematurely grey . . ."

No startling announcement about the continuous creation of other worlds millions of light years away can possibly obviate the fact that our great problem still remains the world in which we live. No journeys to outer space can alter the fact that the most important bit of space, so far as we are concerned, is the ground on which we are standing right now.

During the past decade space-travel has obsessed the imagination of a number of playwrights and novelists, and not a few of them have given their writings a religious motif. Some have depicted the victorious cosmonaut returning to earth in a mood very different from the elation of the two Russians, a dazed and sober mood, because he *did* see God out there. He heard a voice that spoke from the silence of stellar space. The voice said, "Why do you trespass beyond the bounds of your appointed habitation, O vain creature of earth? Must you contaminate my unsullied universe with the stain of your earthly misery and sin? Leave the other worlds to my providence and return to the world that I have given you. That world contains everything essential to your well-being and happiness. To that world I have sent salvation. For that world alone I have given you responsibility."

This is no fiction, but an issue of burning importance that may very well decide the continued existence of the planet earth in the universe. When the President of the United States announced that for the sake of propaganda his nation intended spending from seven to nine billion dollars to send a man on a round trip to the moon before 1970, *The Christian Century*[1] replied editorially that this does not place a high estimate on the intelligence of mankind. It infers that men will follow the system which dazzles, astonishes and intimidates them rather than the system which meets the deepest needs of themselves and their children. This editorial suggested that a finer goal for the United States in the next decade and a worthier object of its astronomical expenditures would be to liberate mankind from fear, hunger, disease, poverty and despair; to promote literacy and opportunity throughout the world, and to strengthen human rights at home and abroad. Let the Russians, with the aid of fireworks craftsmen, escape to the moon if they choose, filling the sky with wonders as they soar into space. But let the concern of the free nations be to fill the empty spaces in men's minds, hearts and stomachs. Let us strive to create a world fit for children to be born in. From such a world no escape will be needed.

That was Christ's mandate to all who believe in him as Son of God and Saviour of the world. After his resurrection he said to the disciples, "Go ye into all the world and preach the Gospel to every creature"; and the Greek word he used here was "oikumene", which does not mean the whole created universe, but the whole inhabited world of men and nations, governments and people, white skins and black skins, poverty and prosperity, tyranny and freedom. Christ gives us responsibility for this world; not for Neptune and Mercury and the Pleiades and the farthest galaxies of outer space, but for this world which is our home, this terrestrial ball which he died to redeem. There is a beautiful story of a Roman Catholic priest in Baltimore who one day saw a small boy bouncing a rubber ball on the pavement. Suddenly a gust of wind blew the ball out of control and rolled it into the traffic of the street where it was destroyed. The priest walked up to the sobbing boy, put his arms around him and quieted him. Then he went back to his study and wrote these lines,

> "A little Boy of heavenly birth,
> But far from home today,
> Comes down to find His ball, the Earth,

[1] *The Christian Century*, June 14th, 1961.

That sin had cast away.
O comrades let us one and all
Join in to get Him back His ball!"[1]

We look at Jesus, and we see *a promise*. We see the fulfilment of God's eternal purpose "to unite all things in him, things in heaven and things on earth". We see "the Holy City, new Jerusalem, coming down out of heaven from God, prepared as a bride adorned for her husband"; and we get behind the forms of this pre-scientific imagery to its inner substance—the promise that Christ will establish his Kingdom, not in outer space, not in some distant heaven, not in some remote galaxy that has never known the agony of moral struggle, but here in this vale of tears and laughter, of misery and grandeur, of sin and redemption. "As it is, we do not yet see everything in subjection to him, But we see Jesus . . ." Man is not yet the lord of creation, but Jesus Christ is Lord, and nowhere in this universe, however vast and unknown and terrifying it may be, shall we remove ourselves from the sphere of his Lordship. God has placed all things in subjection to him, and nothing can separate us from his love or pluck us out of his eternal purpose.

[1] As told by Joseph Sizoo in *Preaching Unashamed* (Abingdon Press, New York), p. 85.

6

The Authority of the Bible

I T WAS one of those red-hot arguments on religion where you felt like asking the antagonists, "Is this a private fight, or can anyone join in?" It took place on a street corner in a little prairie town in Western Canada many years ago. I was a student minister there at the time. A number of curious spectators had gathered to watch these two men as they engaged in an impromptu battle of wits. One of them was an itinerant evangelist who had hired the local dance hall for a week of revival meetings, and that day quite by chance he encountered the local agnostic, a lovable old Norwegian bachelor, an intelligent man, well-read and a keen socialist, but altogether unreligious. They went at it hammer and tongs, with the evangelist definitely coming off second-best, much to the delight of the spectators. Like a skilful swordsman the old Norwegian kept backing him into a corner, and each time the evangelist felt himself trapped he reached into the Bible as though for ammunition and began quoting its verses with the rapidity of machine-gun fire. This exasperated the old Norwegian, and at last he burst out, "You can stop quoting that book at me! I don't believe it anyway!"

It is a fair question to ask, Can we believe the Bible? As you read these chapters in which I attempt to come to grips with certain practical and theoretical obstacles in the path of Christian belief, you can hardly fail to notice that all my insights are drawn from the Bible, as though somehow the Bible possessed a unique authority. By *itself*, however, the Bible poses an obstacle to a great many people, as it did to the old Norwegian bachelor. At once they ask, What gives this Book such superior authority? To be sure, our grandfathers revered the Bible, as men did for three hundred years before them. To them the Bible was the inspired Word of God, every chapter, every phrase, every punctuation mark inerrantly dictated by God and dictated in a sixteenth-century translation. On matters of faith and doctrine the Bible was the final court of appeal. In your doubts you simply consulted the Bible, and whatever the Bible said you could accept without question and without proof.

> "Jesus loves me, this I know,
> For the Bible tells me so."

But all that has changed now—not the love of Jesus but the written authority for it. The Church itself with its work of Higher Criticism has exploded the myth of Scriptural infallibility forever. So if the Bible is no longer considered to be infallible, how can it possibly be authoritative?

At the very outset we ought not to confuse authority with infallibility, because the two terms do not mean the same thing. To call a person or an institution or a book "infallible" means that it contains no possibility of error on any subject, and the Bible certainly does not make that outlandish claim for itself. In fact, the Bible makes no claims for itself. How could it? The Bible is not a book but a collection of books, a veritable library of stories, poems, sermons, biographies, histories and letters written over a period of a thousand years by hundreds of people who never had the slightest idea that their writings would be gathered between the same covers for a specific religious purpose. The Bible is full of mistakes, full of inconsistencies, statements that contradict each other, diverse accounts of the same event and conflicting interpretations of the same truth. People who still call the Bible infallible are claiming for this human collection of books something that the Bible does not claim and has never claimed for itself. We must not confuse the authority of the Bible with infallibility.

We must also mark out the specific areas of life where the Bible does have authority. Science is not one of those areas. The popular play, *Inherit the Wind*, dramatizes humorously and tragically the notorious Scopes trial which took place in the Southern United States some thirty years ago. It concerns a school teacher summoned to court for questioning in his classroom the literal interpretation of the opening chapters of *Genesis.* At one point in the dialogue the defending attorney, who impersonates the great agnostic, Clarence Darrow, produces a rock which he claims to be millions of years old. His opponent, who impersonates the pious

69

politician, William Jennings Bryan, protests that the rock cannot be more than six thousand years old, because Bishop Usher proved conclusively that Creation itself occurred only in the year 4004 B.C.—to be precise, on the 23rd October in the year 4004 B.C. at 9 a.m. Whereupon Darrow throws the court into gales of laughter by asking sarcastically, "Was that Eastern Standard Time? It wasn't Daylight Saving Time, was it? Because the Lord didn't make the sun until the fourth day."[1]

We make Biblical truth a thing to be ridiculed when we literalize it to a point of absurdity. Written in a pre-scientific age, the Bible is not a textbook on geology, nor in some instances does it presume to give an accurate historical record. At the same time we ought never to underrate the historical value of these ancient documents. In one corner of the British Museum you will find a glass case containing the *Codex Sinaiticus*, the oldest complete manuscript of the Bible, written in Greek about the middle of the fourth century; and if you open it at the prophecy of Jeremiah, you will read of the siege of Jerusalem about 700 B.C. by Sennacherib, King of Assyria. Elsewhere in the British Museum you will find another glass case containing a six-sided baked clay cylinder inscribed by Sennacherib's historians, confirming the Bible record exactly and telling how the Assyrian king boasted of having shut up Hezekiah in Jerusalem "like a bird in a cage". It is important in reading the Bible, first, to distinguish between myth and legend and history just as we do in all ancient documents, and second, to realize that myth and legend have equal power with history as vehicles of the truth about God. That forms the subject matter of all the books of the Bible—the truth about God. Its theme is God. It begins with God, continues with God and ends with God in a way that is true of no other collection of writings in the world's literature. In that sense we describe the Bible as the Word of God, and on that subject the Bible has authority.

There must be such authority. One of the most heroic personalities in the Second World War and one of the most victoriously Christian personalities since the war has been Group Captain Leonard Cheshire, V.C., who established his

[1] Jerome Lawrence and Robert E. Lee (reprinted by arrangement with Random House of Canada Ltd., New York and Toronto).

remarkable nursing homes for the care of the incurably ill and the victims of concentration camps. After a tortuous spiritual pilgrimage Cheshire became a Roman Catholic, and he explains quite reasonably the logic of his decision. He says, "If God exists and has spoken to us, then the facts he has revealed to us are no more capable of private interpretation than the facts, say, of aerodynamics." He goes on to say, "When I became a pilot I had to learn the laws of aerodynamics and went to a training school with the authority to teach me. There I expected and found teachers to give me the facts—not their own personal ideas." Cheshire believed that if in every other department of life we submit to the discipline of infallible truth, why should we not expect to do the same thing in that most important department of religion which embraces all life? If the human mind accepts the lesser dogmas of science revealed in supposedly infallible textbooks, what is so odious and degrading in accepting religious truths revealed by God to an infallible Church?[1]

We may protest against the idea of an infallible Church or against any absolute claim made for a relative reality, but we must certainly agree with Cheshire that on religion, of all subjects, we need a more than relative authority. Some people have a curiously distorted idea of religion. They regard it as the supreme sport for amateurs, the one thing in life where expert knowledge counts for nothing, where one man's opinions are quite as good as the next and where anybody is competent to criticize and pass judgment. On all other matters, science for example, the science of the human body or the science of the human mind, the science of physics, biology, astronomy or sociology, they will readily submit to authority, but on the science of God they rate no authority higher than their own individual conscience. This explains, of course, why their religious experience is such a fragile structure, so vulnerable to every wind that blows and so quick to crumble under the strain of suffering, cynicism and persecution. There may be religions in the world that rest on nothing more than a vague personal philosophy and mysticism, but Christianity is not one of them, and remember that we are attempting to scale obstacles to *Christian* belief. As Cheshire said, "If God exists and has spoken to us . . ."

[1] As told by Andrew Boyle in *No Passing Glory* (Collins Fontana Books, London, 1959), p. 328.

Christianity believes exactly that. It is a religion rooted in the Word of God, God's mighty acts in Creation, in Providence and in Redemption, not in ideas that we might form but in something that God has done, realities objective to us, and in those realities we must have authority.

Reformed Protestantism finds that objective authority in the Bible, the written Word of God. There is not a simpler yet more eloquent symbol of the Reformation heritage than the interior of St. Peter's Cathedral in Geneva. A stately Gothic structure, it once contained all the costly and elaborate ornamentation of any European cathedral. But what a difference today! Gone the glittering candles, the incense, the images; instead a pure and holy simplicity. And there in the chancel where the high altar once stood an ordinary table now stands, and on the table one object—an open Book. But we miss the significance of the open Bible if we assume it merely to symbolize the free and unfettered right of Christian people to read a Book which prior to the sixteenth century was closed to them. The open Bible symbolizes not freedom but authority, an authority higher than the Church itself, that objective authority beyond the Church's life through which God speaks to the Church, judges the Church and corrects its whole existence. Protestantism does not idolize the Bible; it has not replaced the living Pope with a paper Pope, an infallible man with an infallible book; but Protestantism does recognize that on the truth of the saving acts of God in history we must have some objective authority beyond the individual conscience, and that authority is the written Word of God.

With right instinct the Church traditionally observes the Second Sunday in Advent as Universal Bible Sunday, giving voice to the historic and familiar collect:

"Blessed Lord, who hast caused all holy scriptures to be written for our learning: Grant that we may in such wise hear them, read, mark, learn, and inwardly digest them, that by patience, and comfort of thy holy Word, we may embrace, and ever hold fast the blessed hope of everlasting life, which thou hast given us in our Saviour Jesus Christ."

Martin Luther described the Bible as "The Manger of Christ", meaning that just as the shepherds and wise men, looking through the eyes of faith, encountered God's In-

72

carnate Word in a manger of straw, so do we through the eyes of faith encounter that same Word in a manger of paper and print. "The Manger of Christ"—when we understand that phrase we shall understand what is meant by the authority of the Bible.

To understand the authority of the Bible we have to distinguish between facts and events in history. As a *fact* the Second World War took place between the years 1939 and 1945, and it included the invasion of Poland and Norway, the fall of France, the Battle of Britain, the bombing, the casualties, D-Day, the liberation of Europe and the end of the Third Reich. As an *event* the Second World War goes back much further and comprises all those blunders in diplomacy which humiliated Germany and set the stage for the rise of Hitler; it also goes beyond the armistice to include the sufferings, the bereavements and the scars on the souls of men and nations. To understand the event of the Second World War we must know something of the history leading up to it and the history following it. We must also have the first-hand account of eye-witnesses, people who saw the event and were involved in it. A century from now some great Oxford historian might prepare a monumental study of the Second World War, but however exhaustive and scholarly, his account would not be as authoritative and authentic as the account of one British soldier who fought with the Allied forces and whose family was killed in the "blitz". That man's account is more than a historical record of the event; it is so close to the event and so bound up in it as to be a part of the event itself.

In that sense we can speak about the authority of the Bible. At the heart and centre of Christianity is a *fact*, the fact of the Incarnation, God's eternal Word becoming flesh and dwelling among us full of grace and truth. As an *event*, however, the Incarnation goes back much further to include the centuries of expectation and preparation in the religious, moral and cultural character of the Jewish people—all of which we learn by reading their sacred writings, their liturgical codes, histories, myths, legends, prophecies, poetry and proverbs in the Old Testament. The Old Testament belongs in the Christian Bible because it points to Christ, it is the prophetic witness to Christ; and we can no more begin the Bible with the coming of Christ and ignore the Old

73

Testament than we can begin one of Shakespeare's plays with its climax in the Third Act and ignore the preparatory scenes which precede it. The Incarnation having taken place, however, neither is there any understanding of it apart from its impact upon those who witnessed it. Without this witness, writes Emil Brunner, "the story of Jesus would not have become a revelation to humanity. It would not have become the Word of God. It would have echoed and re-echoed like a sound which passes unheard in a primeval forest. It would have been like a bridge which had been begun from one side of a river but which had never reached the other side." There is such a witness, however, the personal, first-hand account, committed to writing, of men who lived so close to the event of God's revelation in Christ, who were so involved in it and bound up in it that their witness, their apostolic witness, becomes a part of the event itself. Very early in its history the Church decided to compile a select body of writings, all of which were apostolic in their origin and which would express once and for all in as pure a form as possible the original story of our Lord's life and death and resurrection as well as the impact on the lives of those who witnessed it. No subsequent Christian documents, however scholarly, no Church tradition or papal pronouncement, and certainly no theosophical or mystical speculation can possibly be as authentic and authoritative as the Gospels and Epistles of the New Testament. The *fact* of Christianity is the Incarnation; the *event* is the Incarnation plus prophecy plus witness plus interpretation in the Bible.

From a practical viewpoint, no difficulties involved in reading the Bible can possibly compare with the difficulties of those who cease to read it. In its early years Christianity began to totter, as it is tottering today, under the impact of paganism, atheism and heresy, but as Paul warned young Timothy — religious enthusiasm and morality alone prove a very fragile defence against the enemies of the Faith. Christian experience has but one impregnable foundation, and that is a solid grounding in the written Word of God.

"But continue thou in the things which thou hast learned and hast been assured of, knowing of whom thou hast learned them; And that from a child thou hast known the holy scriptures, which are able to make thee wise unto salvation through faith which is in Christ Jesus. All scripture is given by inspiration of God, and

74

is profitable for doctrine, for reproof, for correction, for instruction in righteousness: That the man of God may be perfect, throughly furnished unto all good works." (2 Timothy 3:14–17)

This is equally true for the Church. Where the Church has lost touch with the Bible, where it has subordinated Scripture to ecclesiasticism, theological tradition and liberal humanism, the Church has wandered from the Gospel into paths of its own devising and has become weak, irrelevant and corrupt. Where the Church has renewed its contact with the Bible, where it has returned to a new and deep study of Scripture, it has found its way back to essential Christianity and to a renewal of its own strength and purpose. It is a matter of history that the giants of the Faith, like Augustine, Luther, and Karl Barth in our own day, can trace the beginnings of their prodigious influence to a rediscovery of the authority of the Bible. It is a matter of history that all the great revivals, reformations and awakenings which have taken place in the life of the Church can be traced, almost without exception, to the same source. When a Church rediscovers the authority of the Bible it is saved from the solitude and self-centredness of a sterile monologue and driven constantly to that radical self-criticism which alone is repentance unto life.

Looking at the Gospel story itself, there is one incident which, more than any other, throws light on what we mean by the authority of the Bible. It takes place in the late afternoon of the first Easter Day. Christ is risen and is abroad in a springtime world, but many of his followers do not know it. Here in the twenty-fourth chapter of Luke's Gospel we see two of them dejectedly trudging their weary way from Jerusalem to Emmaus. Suddenly a stranger catches up with them. They do not recognize him as the risen Christ, and the conversation goes, in effect, like this: "Why are you so depressed?" "Because we thought our Master to be the Messiah, the Saviour of Israel; but now he has been crucified, so, of course, we were mistaken." "Why do you suppose you were mistaken in thinking your Master to be the Messiah?" "Because of the Scriptures. They tell us plainly that the Messiah will come in great glory and power, crushing his enemies beneath his feet." "Are you sure you understand the Scriptures? What about this prophecy from Isaiah, 'He is despised and rejected of men, a man of sorrows and acquainted

75

with grief"? To whom does the prophet allude?" "To Israel, of course." "But is it not true that the ideal Israel comes to perfection in the Messiah? Has it not been foretold that just as Israel must achieve her glory through suffering, so Israel's Messiah must walk the same painful road and that, therefore, it is not only possible but inevitable that he should suffer?" So we are told that the hearts of these two disciples burned within them as the living Christ "opened their minds to understand the Scriptures".

Notice three things about this Emmaus Road incident. First, it establishes the Lordship of Christ over the writings which bear witness to him. We Protestants look to the Bible as our authority, but not as our supreme authority; we do not rate the Book of the Lord higher than the Lord of the Book. There is a kind of Bibliolatry which gets the order reversed and which gives to the written Word of God, usually in a sixteenth-century translation, a higher worship than to God himself. Those who hold this view believe that the Bible as God's Word is not only definitive but terminal. Whatever God intends to say to the human race he has already said. "It's in the Book," there for everyone to read—a view which, carried to its logical extreme, makes God himself no longer necessary. Such Bibliolaters would obviously rather have God as a pen-pal than as a personal companion. The Emmaus Road incident, however, sets the relationship straight. It shows us that while the Bible bears authoritative witness to God's mighty acts in history and is therefore a constant source of knowledge and a means of grace, yet the Bible itself is no substitute for our knowledge and love of God in the living present.

Notice also that our authority on the Christian Faith and life is not Scripture by itself, but Scripture interpreted by Christ, which means two things: that the partial revelation must be read always in the light of the total revelation, and that in order to be understood the Bible has to be read through the eyes of faith. I should urge any man who intends to study the Bible seriously to begin with those four books called Gospels, then to move forward into the New Testament and then backward into the Old Testament. In other words, read every part of the Bible either as a recollection of or an anticipation of that Divine climactic event at its heart and centre, and all its teaching about God in the light of what you know about God through his full revelation in Christ. It is important, moreover, to read the Bible in a Christian perspective. The man outside the Church will, of course, be baffled by the discrepancies in Scripture and he will stumble over many passages in the Old Testament which quite frankly seem contrary to the spirit of Christ, but let him be guided by the Master's warning to those literalists of his own time, "You search the scriptures, because you think that in them you have eternal life; and it is they that bear witness to me; yet you refuse to come to me that you may have life." It takes more than intelligence to understand the Bible; it takes faith, belief in the Lord Jesus and surrender to his spirit. You must read with the soul as well as with the mind. Martin Luther expressed it eloquently when he said that a simple scullery maid reading the Bible in faith comes closer to its message than the greatest scholar reading without faith.

The most important truth we learn from the Emmaus Road incident is that Christ does employ Scripture as a means of revealing the truth about himself. While we are thinking about the authority of the Bible, let us remember that authority can be of two kinds, coercive and moral, and that both of these have been tried in religion as well as in politics. There is nothing coercive about the authority of the Bible — a man may accept it or he may reject it — but to those who read the Bible with unprejudiced and receptive minds the Bible does have a spiritual authority. We believe in the authority of the Bible because men have found it to be authoritative; they have found that it communicated to them the truth about Christ and brought them into fellowship with Christ as in no other way. It is not a dead Christ that we worship but a risen, living Christ whose presence brings us the power of God unto salvation, but the living Christ is the historic Christ, and apart from the Bible no encounter with the historic Christ could take place. Apart from the Bible Christianity is nothing more than a vague, unregenerate mysticism in no way related to that concrete revelation which is the very foundation and the constitutive principle of our faith. We are not asked to *believe* in the authority of the Bible; we are asked to *discover* it in our own experience, as indeed we shall discover it if we surrender ourselves to the beauty and majesty and judgment and

77

comfort and sublime spiritual truth of the written Word of God.

There was another Norwegian who had an experience of the Bible very different from that of the old agnostic bachelor in the Canadian prairie town. Bishop Eivind Berggrav, late Primate of the Lutheran Church in Norway, spent most of the war in a Nazi concentration camp. Before he died in 1959 he wrote a magazine article entitled "What the Bible Means to Me". He tells us that he had always read the Bible, but it was not until the war years when all else had failed him and he turned to the Scriptures with a desperate faith, that he found Christ in its pages. When the Nazis first invaded Norway, the people were bewildered and frightened. Searching for a Word to hearten his congregation on the following Sunday, Bishop Berggrav turned to John's Gospel and was struck by this: "Let not your heart be troubled; believe in God, believe also in me." Later, the Nazis arrested him. As he rode in the car, seated between two policemen, he reached for his pocket Testament and opened it at the First Letter of Peter. Never, he tells, did he experience such a change of mind as he read in the Norwegian version, "Be not afraid of the terror; neither be troubled, but sanctify Christ, the Lord of your heart." He sat in the car praying that Christ would become sanctified in his heart. When they took him before the court, he had a calm mind; he felt safe. During his imprisonment, three full years, the Bible never left him alone. He admits that the crisis sometimes was so strong that the Book seemed to give him no solution, no hope. In such a black mood one day he got the idea to read aloud. Seemingly there was no effect at all, but one hour later he noticed how his mood had changed; confidence had returned; Christ had visited his weak son. "Why aloud?" asks Bishop Berggrav. "I don't know," he replies, "but I think the sound of the voice was like the incarnation of the printed Word and that I had physically acted in faith." This great saint of the Church concludes his article by saying, "To me the Bible is a shrine, *the* shrine of my life. If there is not *exclusively* the gold of God in it, *the gold is there* and it is for *me* and it is to be found nowhere else in the world."

7

The Incredibility of Miracles

IN THE minds of many people the really great obstacle blocking their spiritual pilgrimage is the necessity of believing in miracles. They will go along with Christian truth up to a certain point. Religion as a system of ethics or even as a practice of mystical devotion appeals to them, and they identify themselves with the Church, readily agreeing that historic Christianity plays a tremendously important role as a stabilizing and cohesive force in the life of man and society. If Christianity means being a follower of Jesus Christ, if it means living his life and observing his teachings and supporting his cause, then such people would call themselves Christians. When religion veers over into the realm of the supernatural, however, when the answer to prayer is construed as crude interference in the internal affairs of the law-abiding universe, they mutter something about magic and superstition and promptly part company with their more pious brethren. Ask them their opinion of the New Testament miracles, and they will express honest doubt as to the historical accuracy of these fantastic stories; or admitting their accuracy, they will say that the New Testament miracles were really not so very wonderful because they now have a perfectly natural explanation; or even if they were miraculous, they belong to a unique and unrepeatable situation. Whatever marvellous phenomena may have taken place at the inception of Christianity, the day of miracles is over. There is no room for the miraculous in this enlightened and scientific age. Matthew Arnold was right when he declared dogmatically, "Miracles do not happen!"

May we agree on the definition of miracle as "an occurrence in nature which calls our attention to the work, the purpose and the will of One who is above nature"? In his excellent little book, *The Resurrection of Christ*, where he analyses the Gospel record in the light of recent psychic research, Leslie Weatherhead defines miracle as "a law-

79

abiding event by which God accomplishes his purposes through the release of energies which are normal on a plane of being higher than any with which we are familiar."[1] In all such definitions the important thing is not whether God works within his own laws or outside of them, but that God does work and that he works in ways which to us seem beyond the usual operations of nature. On his own initiative or in answer to prayer God upsets what we understand to be the normal sequence of cause and effect, and to accomplish his purposes God acts in nature, in history and in human life to produce results which would not otherwise be produced. I do not think we can accept anything less than that as a general definition of miracle.

We cannot simply shrug our shoulders when people confess frankly that the need to believe in miracles constitutes a stumbling-block in their spiritual pilgrimage, because that is what Christianity is all about. We must recognize the anomaly of attempting to maintain a structure of Christian experience without the belief in miracles. Here Christianity differs from other ethnic religions. All the essentials of Hinduism would remain unimpaired if you subtracted the miraculous; so with Islam and Buddhism; but Christianity is based on the foundation of miracle, and when you kick away the foundation, the whole structure comes crashing down at your feet. If you have the impulse to go through the Gospels with a pair of scissors cutting away the specific miracle stories which offend your credulity, such as the turning of the water into wine or the feeding of the five thousand or even the accounts of the Resurrection, you may as well throw the rest of the book away, because from cover to cover the New Testament is predicated on a miracle. All the New Testament writers are agreed upon it. "These things are written," said John, "that you may believe that Jesus is the Christ, the Son of God, and that believing you may have life in his name." ". . . that Jesus is the Christ, the Son of God" — not just a good man or a wise teacher or even a prophet, but God incarnate, God clothed in human flesh, God living within our human situation. Is that not the greatest miracle of all, and is it not basic to the whole structure of historic Christianity?

[1] Leslie Weatherhead, *The Resurrection of Christ* (Hodder and Stoughton, London, 1959), p. 26.

Belief in miracle is equally basic to the practice of Christianity. Our whole prayer life rests upon it. In prayer we habitually ask God for miracles, for things which are impossible to us but which, we believe, are not impossible to him, which lie beyond our control but which do not lie beyond his control. Indeed, if we could accomplish these things there would be no need to pray for them. I remember the despair of a woman whose husband had been lost in the bush country for several days. He was on a fishing trip with some other men and managed to get separated from them. You have to know the bush country of northern Canada to understand just how hopeless a situation that can be. They sent out search parties by foot and by airplane, but no trace of him could be found, and eventually we began to fear the worst. Each day I went to visit his anguished wife—they were members of my church—and together we sought God's help in prayer. "It's no use!" she exclaimed after a week of cold weather had gone by, "they will never find him now. There is nothing we can do." I replied, "There is one thing we must do. We must ask God for a miracle." Later, after he had been found and released from the hospital, her husband said, "You know, even in my weakened condition, I never gave up hope. I could almost feel as if I were being prayed for."

We see, then, that belief in miracle is basic to the faith and practice of Christianity. What can be said to the person who finds that belief difficult and to whom it constitutes a stumbling-block in his spiritual pilgrimage? Is there a particular word of God that throws some light on this perplexing problem of the religious life? Consider one of the parables of Jesus—that familiar story of the rich man who in life cared nothing for the beggar at his gate, but in death looked enviously from the torment of hell at the same beggar nestled safely in Abraham's bosom. We must not be satisfied to interpret the parable as a kind of divine "communist manifesto", a proof that the rich will be punished and the poor rewarded beyond the grave, a sort of levelling-off in eternity. That provides only the setting for the story. The main point comes at the end where the rich man asks Abraham to send the beggar back to earth to warn his five brothers against storing up the same punishment for themselves. Abraham replies, "They have Moses and the prophets; let them hear them." "No, father Abraham," says the rich man, "but if someone goes to them from the dead, they will repent." And here comes the punch line as Abraham replies, "If they do not hear Moses and the prophets, neither will they be convinced if someone should rise from the dead."

C. S. Lewis makes that point in his book on *Miracles* where he states that the question, "Do miracles occur?" has no meaning save as we have answered the prior question, "Are miracles possible?" He says that the only person in his experience who claims to have seen a ghost still disbelieves in ghosts even after seeing one. Seeing is not believing; we can always say that we have been the victim of an illusion —for which reason the question of whether miracles occur can never be answered by experience, our own or someone else's. If we have decided to begin with the premise that miracles are impossible, then no amount of personal or historical evidence will convince us otherwise. If we declare categorically, "Miracles do not happen!", then we are wasting our time by studying the records of miracles which are supposed to have happened. If we do not believe that in order to accomplish his purposes God *can* act in nature and history and human life to produce results which would not otherwise be produced, then miracles, when they do take place, are wasted on us, because we shall never recognize them as miracles. As Lewis points out, the philosophical question must come first. "If they do not hear Moses and the prophets, neither will they be convinced if someone should rise from the dead."

This is not theology but history. This thing actually happened, and it happened exactly as the parable predicts. A man did rise from the dead and he appeared to a number of people who had known him during his earthly life. But here is the significant fact: he appeared only to his friends, to Mary in the garden, to the two disciples on the Emmaus Road, to the eleven in the Upper Room, to Peter by the seashore, and to certain others—to those who already believed in him, who loved him and who followed him. He did not appear to his enemies, although the imagination kindles when we visualize him striding into the Jewish Sanhedrin or the Governor's palace or the soldiers' barracks. Imagine the consternation of Caiaphas and Pilate and the Centurion confronted by this man whom they had crucified three days earlier. Would they not have sunk to their knees in terror, blubbering out their repentance and crying aloud for mercy? No, they would not. They would have dismissed the thing as a hallucination or else roared in anger over the failure of the executioners to do their job properly. How, indeed, could they have recognized the risen Christ when many of his own followers failed to recognize him? In literal truth they did not have the spiritual vision to discern the living presence of Jesus. They bear out the Master's own word, "If they do not hear Moses and the prophets, neither will they be convinced if someone should rise from the dead."

Graham Greene develops this very theme in his powerful play, *The Potting Shed*. As the story begins, Mr. Henry Callifer is dying. All the members of the family have been summoned to his bedside except his son, James. James arrives, nevertheless, and though he pleads with his mother, she will not allow him to see his dying father. James, whose marriage and life have been wrecked, so that he cannot now live without psychiatric treatment, does not understand why from his earliest memory he has been treated like an outcast by his own parents. After his father's funeral he determines to find out the reason, and he learns it from his uncle, the Reverend William Callifer, an alcoholic priest. It seems that once in his boyhood James hanged himself in the potting shed in the garden. When the gardener found him, he was dead. He had been dead for some time. There could be no doubt of this; his heart had stopped beating. His uncle, who was there at the time, prayed for the boy, and just as surely as the breath had left his body, so the breath returned, and he regained consciousness. His father did not rejoice, however, because his father had been a very famous free-thinker, an agnostic who wrote many books discrediting religion, disproving the existence of God, debunking Jesus and exploding the myth of immortality. To admit the reality of what had happened in the potting shed would mean the supreme embarrassment of retracting publicly everything that he had said and written. With proof under his nose at the bottom of his own garden, he still refused to believe and chose to destroy his son rather than his own reputation. Henry Callifer bears out the Master's word, "If they do not hear Moses and the prophets, neither will they be convinced if someone should rise from the dead."

Perhaps that explains why Jesus himself was so reticent about performing miracles during his earthly ministry in Galilee and Judea. We read that when the Pharisees tempted him, demanding a sign from heaven, he would not give them a sign. He who possessed the power of God deliberately avoided making displays of supernatural power. Why? Because he knew that they would convince nobody. They might dazzle people and fascinate them for the moment, but in the long run it would be his message, not his miracles that converted men and brought them into the Kingdom of God.

Recall that succession of mighty works recorded in the fifth and sixth chapters of Mark's Gospel, each surpassing in magnitude and intensity the one that preceded it. Over in Gennesaret Jesus restores sanity to a demoniac — a healing miracle. Call it psychological, if you wish, but a remarkable cure nonetheless. Back in Capernaum the Master performs a miracle definitely not psychological. He heals a woman of an organic ailment which for twelve years has baffled the most reputable and expensive physicians. Then he does what no man has ever done before or since. He does the impossible — brings a dead child back to life, proving himself the Master over all nature, with power even to reverse nature's final judgments. After this he goes to Nazareth, his home town, and what is the climax of this ascending series of miracles? The Gospel writer tells us: "He could not do many mighty works there because of their unbelief." Let us get the order correct. People do not believe in Jesus because he does mighty works; rather, he does mighty works because they believe in him. Christianity does not argue from miracle to faith; rather it moves from faith to miracle: and if there is no faith, no prior belief in Jesus, then miracles, even if they happen, are wasted, because we shall not accept them as miracles anyway.

The New Testament writers would have been appalled that future generations should find the Gospel miracles a barrier to belief. They wrote the Gospels for the benefit of believers, and it would seem incredible to them that anyone could accept Jesus as the revelation of God but refuse to accept the record of large areas of his earthly ministry. There is, after all, a certain fitness about the Gospel miracles, an intrinsic probability, a consistency with the character and the mission of him who performed them. They are not fantastic and gruesome like the miracles in *Grimm's Fairy Tales* where men turn into monsters and trees walk and ships become goddesses. Nor are they destructive and useless like some of the Old Testament miracles which seem to belong more to oral legend than to historic fact. The miracles of our Lord form an integral part of his earthly ministry. It is reasonable surely that he who came to make men whole should heal their sick bodies as well as their sick souls; that he who offered the Bread of Life for their spiritual hunger should satisfy physical hunger as well; that he who came to save men from evil should save them from disease and death and all the manifestations of evil's power. Again we must get the order straight, remembering that the Gospels presuppose faith in Jesus and in what he was. The miracles do not authenticate him; he authenticates the miracles.

The same is true of the two great miracles in the New Testament—the Virgin Birth and the Resurrection. As a Protestant I have never considered the Virgin Birth essential to the structure of the Gospel. I go along with Bishop Pike of the Episcopal Church in the United States. When a group of High Church clergymen in Georgia recently accused him of heresy for disbelieving in the Virgin Birth, he suggested that segregation of the black and white races in the Episcopal churches of the South is a "heresy really worth discussing". At the same time it does not seem illogical to me that he who was the Son of God should have been brought into the world by a direct operation of God rather than by the ordinary course of human generation. Nor does it seem illogical that his means of leaving the world should be so extraordinary. We have the Gospel stories which witness to the detailed events of our Lord's resurrection, but even if we did not have these stories—and the *first* Christian converts did not have them—we should know that Jesus, being who he was, the Resurrection had to take place. As Peter said after Pentecost, "God raised him up, having loosed the pangs of death, because it was not possible for him to be held by it."

It is from that point of view that we approach the main question of this chapter: "Can we believe in miracles?" Taken by themselves as isolated occurrences outside the context of religious faith, miraculous events will be lost on us; we shall not even recognize them as purposeful acts of God. When Moses called from heaven a dreadful series of

85

plagues upon the Egyptians he intimidated the cruel Pharaoh, but he did not convert him from paganism to the worship of Jehovah. When Elijah called down fire from heaven to consume the offerings on the heathen altars, he dispersed the priests of Baal, but he did not win them over to the religion of Israel. As Jesus said, "If they do not hear Moses and the prophets, neither will they be convinced if someone should rise from the dead." The Resurrection convinces nobody; it brings us not a step closer to belief in the possibility of miracles unless we have a prior faith in the wisdom, power and love of God. Suppose we possess that faith, however. Suppose we believe that God is and that God is like Jesus. What does that imply for our belief in miracles?

It means that we shall not impose our human limitations upon God. The sceptic will say, "I do not believe in miracles because they are contrary to the laws of nature," but Augustine answered that question centuries ago when he said that miracle is not contrary to nature, but only to what we know of nature. The sceptic will go a step further and say that miracles do not happen because science has revealed nature to be a closed system, cause and consequence joined in an inevitable succession that man cannot break and that God does not break. But has science revealed nature to be a closed system? Surely if there is one place in our modern world where men preserve open minds and refuse to believe that the last word on nature's laws has been spoken, that place is a scientific laboratory. Still undaunted, the sceptic refuses to believe in miracle because he takes nature to be the whole of reality, and he will not admit the existence of any being or power outside or above the world of nature. He forgets that his very act of thinking is an obvious proof of the supernatural. Rational thought is not a product of nature: it transcends nature, it is super-nature, it induces and enables us to alter the course of nature. Therefore, we shall allow God at least the measure of freedom which we allow ourselves. Indeed, if we really believe in him at all, in his creatorhood and sovereignty and power, we shall never commit the blasphemy of prescribing limits for God and of saying what he can do and what he cannot do, else we shall deserve the rebuke delivered to Job: "Shall fault-finders contend with the Almighty? He who argues with God, let him answer it."

86

If we believe that God is and that God is like Jesus, then we shall know that in his scale of values people are more important than laws. "The Sabbath was made for man and not man for the Sabbath," Jesus declared to the Pharisees when they criticized him for violating the regulations governing the Sabbath in order to meet the needs of sick and hungry people. Jesus believed that the most important thing in this world is a human soul and that the whole world cannot be set in the balance over against it. He believed that laws, institutions and regulations are the servants, not the masters, of the human soul, and that they should be modified, changed or waived when they conflict with the soul's welfare. Now nature is not a democracy governed by laws of its own making, laws which brook no interference from its Creator and Sustainer. Nature is a monarchy governed by a Sovereign who, having ordained its laws in the first place, reserves precisely the right to modify, change or waive those laws according to his own purpose. And if nature's Sovereign is like Jesus, if he is a Father as Jesus described and revealed him, then his supreme interest is not in maintaining the inexorable regularity of law in this universe, but in administering these laws to meet what he understands to be the needs of his children.

If God is like Jesus, we shall ask him for miracles in the faith that he will grant them. Where unscalable mountains block our path so that we have come to a dead-end in life's journey, we shall not be afraid to ask God to remove these mountains and cast them into the depths of the sea. We shall not prescribe the precise method in which God will accomplish the impossible for us — God works in his own way — but we shall believe that so long as our faith opens a channel for God to fulfil his purpose through our lives, then the power of God will be a factor in our lives producing results which would not otherwise be produced. In our distress we shall cry to him for material relief, and it will come to us from the most unexpected quarters. In sickness we shall ask for health, and we shall see a cure effected which amazes the doctors. We shall pray for a change of character in someone for whom we care deeply, and in surprising ways our petition will be answered. The question, "Can we believe in miracles?" will have no meaning for us, any more than the question, "Can we believe in jet propulsion?" has meaning for an aeroplane pilot. So far as we are concerned belief in God and belief in miracles belong to the same order of reality, and to live the life of prayer is to live in a world of miracles, miracles only to us perhaps, but still miracles because they are "occurrences in nature which call our attention to the work, the purpose and the will of One who is above nature".

8

The Divinity of Christ

THE Christian festival of Christmas comes once a year, but you need not be especially Christian to join in the celebrations. All sorts of people, with no room in their thinking for a spiritual interpretation of life, look forward to a jolly time at the season of our Saviour's birth. Not that Christ begrudges them their wholesome fun; if the Son of Man brought anything into the world he brought the reasons for goodness and gladness and love and laughter. It is doubtful, however, if Jesus saw the significance of his coming watered down to nothing more than a crisis in human good-will. Yet that has happened to Christmas. This most holy and supernatural event has degenerated into a pagan holi-day, exploited by commercial interests and almost hectically observed by people who are not only indifferent but some-times antagonistic to its sacred origins. As one woman was overheard to remark when she saw a manger-scene in a shop window, "The Church again! Now it's trying to horn in on Christmas!" There has grown up in our day a sort of *Christmas-in-General*, a complex pattern of customs and traditions without the slightest reference to or dependence upon its religious content.

If one were permitted to enunciate a law, after the manner of Professor Parkinson, it would be this: Society observes *Christmas-in-Particular* in inverse proportion to its observance of *Christmas-in-General*. The more hectic and complex our involvement in the secular by-products of Christmas, the less time or interest we have in the fact which Christmas supposedly celebrates. Indeed the Church has reached a point where it almost desperately pleads with people to give Christ at least a look-in on the festival of his own birth. A few years ago the drama critic of a London newspaper, not a churchgoer himself, told of receiving from his local Parish Church an invitation which struck him as really lamentable in its tone. It read, "Christmas Day is the

89

birthday of our Lord Jesus Christ—Will you let him share it with you in one or more of these services?" "Will I let him!" exploded the critic. "Should I not be told firmly and even fiercely that if I believe in the facts of the Christmas story, then it is a supreme privilege to be allowed to share in this grandeur of spiritual opportunity, and that I am committing unpardonable folly if I miss the chance of sharing such communion?"

Christmas-in-Particular celebrates such an earth-shaking, history-making, soul-transforming fact, that if ever we did grasp its significance we should indeed celebrate it with a new sense of wonder and humility, counting it the supreme privilege to be allowed to share in this grandeur of spiritual opportunity. That fact can be summarized in a few short sentences. Nearly twenty centuries ago a Baby was born to humble parents in faraway Palestine. God was in that Baby. His parents called him Jesus, and when he became a man he travelled the countryside teaching people that God loves them and that they should love one another. God was in that Teacher. This Jesus had miraculous powers from which he ministered to the poor, the sick, the sorrowing, the dispossessed and the sinful. God was in those acts of mercy. He offended the religious authorities, so they crucified him, and he let them do it; he who lived a perfect life and who, had he wished, could have crushed evil out of existence, allowed human sin to murder him on a cross. God was on that Cross. They buried him in a rock-hewn tomb and sealed the mouth of it with a great stone, but three days later he smashed that stone, burst the bonds of death and declared his regnancy forever. God was in that Resurrection. That is what *Christmas-in-Particular* celebrates—the tremendous and staggering truth of the Nicene Creed which asserts that Jesus Christ, born in a Bethlehem stable under the Judean night sky, was "begotten of his Father before all worlds, God of God, Light of Light, Very God of Very God . . . of one substance with the Father". The Apostle Paul expressed it more simply when he wrote to the Corinthians, "God was in Christ."

But this is not a simple fact to understand. Men have always had difficulty grasping and holding on to what we call the truth of the Divinity of Christ; and while we are still attempting to scale certain obstacles in the path of Christian belief, we must certainly face up squarely to the most baffling obstacle of all. "God was in Christ"—some of us take that for granted; we regard it as axiomatic, the very foundation-stone of Christianity; but as the writer of *First Peter* states very clearly, it is "a stone that will make men stumble, a rock that will make them fall". Unitarianism emerged in Europe and America as an attempt to preserve the ethical and mystical side of Christianity without the straitjacket of dogma, an attempt to revere the historic Jesus as hero, martyr and teacher without believing that he was God. Many liberal Protestants, though they might not shout it aloud from the roof-tops, have essentially the Unitarian viewpoint; while others remain outside the Church, because the moment they try to enter they stumble over this foundation-stone of Christ's Divinity. They believe in God and they believe in Jesus. They believe what Jesus taught about God and they believe that Jesus was God-inspired, but that is as far as they will go. When the Church begins to identify God and Jesus, claiming for Christ a more-than-human-status, these people shake their heads and walk sorrowfully away.

So let us look squarely at the meaning of *Christmas-in-Particular*, the Apostle's claim that "God was in Christ". Let us approach this obstacle of Christ's Divinity by asking three questions: First, what are we asked to believe? Second, what are the bases of this belief? Third, does it matter if we hold this belief?

I

First, what are we asked to believe? We must decide that, because many people who say that they believe in the Divinity of Christ are not at all sure what they are believing, while others who say that they disbelieve the Divinity of Christ are not at all sure what they are disbelieving. The Bible declares emphatically that God was in Christ, but what does that mean?

Let us be clear that the truth celebrated by *Christmas-in-Particular* is not primarily an assertion about Jesus, but about God. Ordinarily we presuppose a certain knowledge of God, of God's character and personality, his ways and works, his will and purpose, his grace and truth, and, holding in our minds a picture of what we believe God to be like, we put Jesus alongside that picture and try to measure the family resemblance. We try to settle our doubts by deciding whether Jesus is really like God. If we were honest we should reverse the order and realize that all we know about God with any certainty we have learned from Jesus. Christianity does not look from God to Jesus; rather it looks from Jesus to God; and it is a real question whether, apart from Jesus, we should be able to form any clear picture of God at all.

Karl Barth has written, "What God is and what it is to be Divine is something that we can learn only where God has revealed himself." Barth means that we can never know God directly; we can never make him an object of study in the sense that we make the human body or the earth's minerals or the stars in their courses an object of study; we can never reach up to heaven and by philosophy or mystic contemplation search out and find God and grow in the knowledge of him. We have knowledge of God only because God graciously gives us that knowledge; he reveals himself, he shows us what he is like and he does this through the phenomena of our own experience, through objects and events which in themselves are not God but are transparent to God. Men have looked at the world of nature, through a telescope at the myriads of stars and through a microscope at the complex beauty of a living organism, and they have seen in its majesty and orderliness the signature of an intelligent Creator. Men have looked back over the process of history and they have discerned the evidence of a more than human Power giving coherence to the process, working for the dethronement of evil and the enthronement of righteousness. Men have looked into their own hearts and have felt there a Presence that disturbed them with the joy of elevated thoughts, a longing, a hunger and a constraint which the things of earth could not satisfy.

All of these are revelations of God, they point to God, but have they taught us all that we believe about God? What, in fact, do we believe? That God is personal, that the living, pulsating, creative Spirit at the heart and centre of this universe has all the characteristics of what we understand as personality. He is a self-conscious Being, conscious of other beings. He thinks, he knows, he feels, he understands, he loves, he hates, he mourns, he rejoices. "So the all-powerful were all-loving too," and when we speak of God we speak not of *It* but of *Him*. We have to do with *Him*, we can pray to *Him*, we can expect *Him* to answer our prayers, to take sides, to have purposes and preferences. Supremely we believe that God is personal, but what assurance have we of its truth unless God has revealed himself through personality? Only personality can reveal personality. All that we know with any certainty about God we have learned from Jesus; everything that we believe about the personality and the character of God rests on the foundation of the Divinity of Christ.

The man *inside* the Church who secretly doubts the Divinity of Christ would call himself a heretic, though oddly enough the earliest heresy in the history of our Faith was a denial of our Lord's humanity. The Docetists believed that Jesus was God, but they did not believe that he was fully and completely man. We marvel at this in view of the very human figure who emerges from the pages of the Gospels, a man among men whose humanity is unmistakable and authentic. His body was flesh and blood like ours with its capacity for pain, privation and fatigue. As a child he was subject to his parents, and like other children he grew "in wisdom and in stature and in favour with God and man". His emotional life revealed the shifting play of love and wonder and anger and compassion and sorrow. His moral experience took him into the wilderness of temptation, his social instincts led him to crave the company of friends, and his spiritual needs found him in the house of worship and the place of prayer. The Bible tells us that "the Word was made flesh", and it uses the term "flesh" to emphasize the completeness of God's incarnation in a human personality, all that nature of man in which he could grow, learn, struggle, be tempted, suffer and die.

There was a Hindu who had investigated and rejected Christianity. He could not believe that Infinite God would become man. But one day in a pasture he became interested in a colony of ants. As he bent over, his shadow fell across the ant hill. Immediately there was confusion among the insects — workers dropped their burdens, warriors appeared to defend the city, and panic reigned. As the man drew back, the sun fell again on the ant hill and order was gradually restored. But as he bent over it again, the fleeting patterns of panic reappeared. Idly he began to wonder how he could bridge the gap between man and the insect, to show the ants that his drawing near indicated nothing but sympathy and interest. The pondering became strangely intense until the idea gripped him that the only way this would be possible would be somehow to become an ant himself, accepting the risks and terrors of life in the sand and grass; only then could be communicated to the insects the intentions of his human heart. Bent in the dust, he had been thinking God's thoughts after him. Now he understood the meaning of the Incarnation.

"God was in Christ reconciling the world unto himself" —that is the Christian Gospel and that is the truth which *Christmas-in-Particular* celebrates. The Divinity of Christ means that the invisible God, of whose person we catch only a fleeting glimpse in nature and history and conscience, has once and for all come where we are, clothed himself in our flesh, made our situation his situation, our perils his perils, and revealed himself to us clearly and unmistakably in terms that we can best understand. "No one has ever seen God; the only Son, who is in the bosom of the Father, he has made him known." "For in him the whole fulness of the deity dwells bodily." That is what we are asked to believe —that God was in Christ.

II

Second, we must ask, What are the bases of our belief in the Divinity of Christ? As an article of faith it did not originate with the speculations of later theologians. Let us be clear on that point. Certain doctrines of the Church do have their origins in the minds of men—for example, the Church's teaching about purgatory and the geography of the afterlife, its teaching about transubstantiation and apostolic succession—and though we shall not take issue with these doctrines which obviously bind believers to God, yet we can understand that for many people they constitute barriers to belief because they are the product of man-made theologies. Other doctrines are different, however. They have their roots not in speculative theology but in the personal, first-hand experience of the men who wrote the New Testament. Such a doctrine is the Divinity of Christ.

94

Picture the scene in first-century Palestine—the whole country agog over the appearance of a unique and startling personality, Jesus of Nazareth. He goes through the cities and villages talking to little groups of people about God and the good life and the Kingdom of God, preaching a doctrine quite contradictory to that preached by other religious teachers of his day. He performs marvellous miracles, gives sight to the blind, cleanses lepers, makes lame people walk and even brings the dead back to life. Everybody is talking about him. He is the number one topic of conversation. Everybody tries to figure out who and what he is. Some say that he may be John the Baptist risen from the grave, or a reincarnation of Elijah or Jeremiah or one of the other great Jewish prophets. He has gathered around him a small group of disciples to help him in his ministry and one day, sensing their perplexity, he asks them point-blank, "Who do men say that I am?" They tell him the popular rumours. Then he asks the more pointed question, "But who do you say that I am?" There and then, perhaps under the shade of a tree at the side of a country road, the doctrine of the Divinity of Christ is promulgated. Speaking for all the disciples, these men who have lived close to Jesus and shared his feelings and purposes from the beginning, Peter replies, "You are the Christ, the Son of the living God!"

The disciples of Jesus did not come easily and quickly to that conclusion, nor was it shared by many outside the apostolic group. Quite the contrary, in fact. The religious authorities had no argument with Jesus as a teacher and faith-healer, but because he committed the crowning blasphemy of claiming to be divine, they nailed him to a cross and jeered at him to prove the truth of his Divinity. Those who knew him best, however, could draw no other conclusion than that articulated by Peter, "You are the Christ . . ." They tried to explain him as something less, as prophet, teacher, leader, good man, but none of these categories sufficed. We can almost imagine the evolution of their knowledge. At first they may have said that *God sent him*, but that sounded too cold, as though God were a bow and Jesus the arrow; that would not do. Then they said, *God is with him*. That went deeper, yet as their experience of him progressed, even that seemed inadequate. Finally we catch the reverent accents of a new conviction—*God came in him.* He is God in human form, God made visible and real within our experience. "You are the Christ . . ."

If we ask what brought the disciples to this amazing conclusion we must certainly consider the claims that Jesus made for himself—immense claims such as no one has made before or since. He called God his Father and himself God's Son, but he left no doubt that the relationship between God and himself was something more intimate and divine than that between an earthly parent and his child. "I and the Father are one," he told the Pharisees. And when Philip in the Upper Room said wistfully, "Lord, show us the Father, and we shall be satisfied," Jesus answered with tender patience, "Have I been with you so long, and yet do you not know me, Philip? He who has seen me has seen the Father." What shall we make of this claim? As one person has said, "Either it is the infatuation of an absurd megalomania, or else it is really true. Either these sayings are the preposterous, incredible arrogance of a pathetic and pathological egotism —or else he had a right to say them." The writers of the New Testament believed that Jesus did have a right to say them.

They believed that because, so far as they could see, everything about Jesus validated his claims. On the lips of any other man they would, of course, have been sheer blasphemy, but when Jesus claimed not only to bring the truth about God but to *be* the truth about God, they believed him, because coming from him the claim had a certain fitness. They knew that something more than a human spirit dwelt within this man whose very presence brought into time the aroma of eternity. It was not what he said about God but the fact that he himself seemed so Godlike, so altogether human, yet so altogether Divine. Though possessed of all the manly instincts and impulses, he had absolutely no trace of evil about him. Evil assaulted him more fiercely than it assaults any man, but neither in his body nor his spirit could evil find lodgment. Everything they had ever surmised about the purity, the holiness, the justice, the kindness and the compassion of God seemed incarnate in this man who was bone of their bone and flesh of their flesh, and looking at him the disciples found themselves looking through him to a revelation of something eternally true about God.

Moreover, they saw that beyond what he said and what

he was, Jesus did things that only God could do. Specifically he forgave sins, and even now whoever commits a gross violation of the moral law knows that he can never be right in his own conscience or right with his fellow men until he is right with God, and that means that God has to make him right by forgiving him. When four men made a hole in a roof and lowered a bed bearing a paralytic at the feet of Jesus, he said to the poor fellow, "My son, your sins are forgiven." That shocked some of the bystanders. "Why does this man speak thus?" they muttered among themselves. "It is blasphemy! Who can forgive sins but God alone?" Now the point is that the disciples agreed with them one hundred per cent. They believed implicitly that only God can forgive sins. But see what happens. This thing which none but God can do — this divine, supernatural thing — Jesus *does*, and he does it again and again, as in the case of the paralytic who, released from the crippling chains of guilt, rises from his bed and walks home.

So we see that the conviction of the New Testament writers about the Divinity of Christ grew out of their experience, as indeed it must grow out of every man's experience. Some people declare indifferently or even truculently that they do not believe in Christ, but then, they are not competent to believe in Christ; they have no qualifications for believing in him, no possibility of understanding the fact of his Divinity because they have not yielded themselves in faith to that fact. They are like Simon the Pharisee who reacted with disgust at the sight of an ex-prostitute pouring precious ointment over the feet of Jesus simply because, never having surrendered himself to the power of God in Christ, he could not understand the motives behind this extravagant act of devotion. From outside a church a stained-glass window looks ugly and meaningless; you have to step inside the church to appreciate the artistry, the beauty and the inspiration of the window. Christ is like that. Outside the community of faith he may indeed seem nothing more than a good man or even the best of men; but inside that community the light of heaven shines through him, and with the apostle of old we cry out in loving adoration, "My Lord and my God!"

Now we must ask, Does it matter if we believe in the Divinity of Christ? There can be only one answer—Nothing matters more, if we wish to build and preserve a structure of Christian faith and experience. Imagine a great cathedral in process of construction. It has taken years to build, and so far only the nave can be used as a place of worship. The transepts and towers and side-chapels will be added as funds become available, but there is no hurry, because the foundations have been well and truly laid and they will support the most massive structure as it rises to completion. A man's faith is like that cathedral. It cannot rise to completion in a single day, and there are many adornments and extras which need not concern him greatly because they will be added in due time as he pays the price of understanding and study. There are also the foundation beliefs, however, those basic and constitutive doctrines which must be laid at the very beginning, because upon them the whole structure of Christian Faith and experience rests. Such is the Divinity of Christ— more than a foundation; the very corner-stone that holds the building together. "For no other foundation can any one lay than that which is laid, which is Jesus Christ."

Certainly the New Testament is predicated on this belief. The New Testament is a historical record, as authentic as any other collection of ancient documents, and the figure in its pages is as much a historic person as Caesar or Socrates; but the New Testament does not pretend to be an impartial record. It is the most biased book in the world and was written after the event of God's revelation in Christ by men who believed the event of God's revelation in Christ. See how the earliest Gospel-writer starts his biography of Jesus: "The beginning of the Gospel of Jesus Christ, the Son of God." See how the Fourth Gospel ends: "These are written that you may believe that Jesus is the Christ, the Son of God, and that believing you may have life in his name." The thirteen letters of Paul preserved in the New Testament are all written from a single viewpoint—belief in the eternal Son of God "who, though he was in the form of God, did not count equality with God a thing to be grasped, but emptied himself, taking the form of a servant, being born in the

98

likeness of men". Remove the foundation-truth of Christ's Divinity, and though the New Testament remains an interesting museum piece, yet as a living and powerful and saving Word of God the New Testament collapses.

When Sadhu Sundar Singh, a distinguished Indian convert to Christianity, was asked by a sceptical professor what new thing he found in Christianity which his former religion did not possess, he replied, "Jesus Christ." When pressed further with the question, "What new idea or principle have you found in your new religion?", he said, "Jesus Christ." In the Sadhu's own country, India, and in its capital city, New Delhi, the Third General Assembly of the World Council of Churches met in November 1961, to reaffirm its faith in *Jesus Christ the Light of the World*, not the Light of Europe or America but the Light of the *World*, and not one light among many others but *The Light*, the only Light that God has given to relieve the darkness of man's confusion and despair. Nineteen centuries of Christianity are predicated on the belief that "the God who said, 'Let light shine out of darkness,' has shone in our hearts to give the light of the knowledge of the glory of God in the face of Christ". Not in loyalty to a crucified carpenter nor with a passion to propagate his teaching, but in loyalty to a Divine Saviour and with a passion to propagate his Gospel, the saints, apostles, martyrs, reformers and missionaries of the ages have built a Church which is still building and which rests upon no other foundation than the belief that "God was in Christ".

There was a day when death had darkened the home of that rugged but sensitive soul, Thomas Carlyle. Someone, taking a New Testament, opened it at the Gospel of John and read the familiar words, "Let not your heart be troubled. In my Father's house are many mansions." "Aye," muttered the bereaved man, "if you were God you had a right to say that; but if you were only a man, what do you know any more than the rest of us?"[1] The same might be said of all the promises of Jesus, all his teachings about God and the Christian life and the Kingdom of God, all his commandments to follow him, all his assurance of salvation in this world and in the world to come. We can believe that the way of life set before us in the Sermon on the Mount, the

[1] As told by James S. Stewart in *The Strong Name* (T. & T. Clark, Edinburgh, 1940), p. 80.

way of love and lowliness and sacrifice, the way of a Cross, is the right way for us to walk, not because a good man or even the best of men pointed it out, but because God himself came where we are and himself walked that way and showed it to us as the path to glory.

Christianity is not a Gospel without the Divinity of Christ. Many years ago in a poor district of Aberdeen, where open-air preaching was common, a Unitarian minister faced the people with his message of Jesus the inspired prophet, matchless teacher and heroic example. After a time these stalwart Scottish folk told the minister that if that was all he had to say, there was really no use in his coming to preach at all. One fallen woman standing near by said to him, "Your rope is not long enough for me." But the Gospel of Christ's Divinity comes as good news to us because it does tell of a rope, a long rope that reaches all the way from heaven and reaches, therefore, with saving power into the deepest pit of our misery and sin. "God was in Christ" — that is the Gospel, the glorious truth of *Christmas-in-Particular*, and we celebrate it with unutterable and exalted joy.

9

The Injustice of God

"If God is God he is not good,
If God is good he is not God."

THAT little couplet comes from Archibald MacLeish's play, "J.B.", which enjoyed a long run in New York, though not in London, and is a modern adaptation of the Biblical drama of *Job*. In writing this play MacLeish was convinced that the times are singularly ripe for a rediscovery of *Job*, this fascinating Old Testament story of a righteous and godly man who suffered excruciating disasters and demanded to know the reason why. A religious periodical quotes MacLeish as saying:

"No man can believe in life itself who does not believe that life can be justified. But how can life be justified in a time in which life brings with it such inexplicable sufferings: a time in which millions upon millions of men and women and children are destroyed and mutilated for no crime but the crime of being born in a certain century or of belonging to a certain race or of inhabiting a certain city: a time in which the most shameless and cynical tyranny flourishes, in which the ancient decencies are turned inside out to make masks for cruelty and fraud, in which even the meaning of the holiest words is perverted to deceive men and enslave them? How can we believe in our lives unless we can believe in the justice of God, and how can we believe in the justice of God in a world in which the innocent perish in vast meaningless massacres, and brutal and dishonest men foul all the lovely things? These are the questions we in our generation ask ourselves..."

No obstacle to Christian belief looms more menacingly than that which the playwright describes as the injustice of God. We open the Bible and we see there a picture of One who is "righteous in all his ways, and holy in all his works"; we look at life and we see a jungle where holiness and righteousness count for nothing: and we ask, "How can the two be reconciled?" Oscar Wilde used to say that there was enough suffering in any lane in London to prove that a good God does not govern the world; lust and pain and sorrow and anxiety and gruelling disappointment. It seems to us that if God were all-powerful, that is, if he were really God, he would not tolerate the existence of innocent suffering; but since it does exist, and never on a wider scale than today, we can only be afraid that there is no all-powerful God, and therefore no God at all. Our problem, simply stated:

"If God is God he is not good,
If God is good he is not God."

The injustice of God becomes a more burning issue in terms of personal experience. Never did any man grapple more passionately with this baffling obstacle to belief than did the writer of the seventy-third Psalm. Tradition identifies him as one Asaph, a famous and brilliant poet and musician of his generation. His name does not matter, though, because Asaph is every man in every generation whose structure of faith groans and totters under the pressure of hard facts and grim reality. His confession of bewilderment echoes our sentiments,

"For I was envious of the arrogant, when I
saw the prosperity of the wicked.
They are not in trouble as other men are;
they are not stricken like other men."

From where he sat it looked to Asaph as if there were no justice in life, no moral order, in fact no order at all. As he saw it, a man could be ruthless, selfish, materialistic and immoral, he could be all kinds of a devil and get away scot-free. Obviously it profited a man nothing to obey God and keep the Ten Commandments, because *he* had been obedient, *he* had been virtuous, *he* had been devout, and *he* had been kicked all over the place like a dog ill-treated by its master.

"All in vain have I kept my heart clean
and washed my hands in innocence.
For all the day long I have been stricken,
and chastened every morning."

It is worthwhile to look at Asaph, because he handled his problem constructively and because he has something very important to teach us about overcoming this obstacle to belief. We notice, for example, that he kept quiet about his difficulty; he chose to work it out by himself rather than share it with people and make it their difficulty too. Why do some men, when their faith begins cracking, shout it aloud from the housetops, or from the television screen, and clamour to get it into print, foisting their doubts, as it were a grudge upon the rising generation? If they cannot believe, they will make sure, by heaven, that nobody else can either! as though they needed public confirmation of their own doubts. An impulse of this kind must have tempted Asaph, but something checked him, for he said, "If I will speak thus, I would have been untrue to the generation of thy children." He pictured his disillusionment becoming universal, an entire generation growing up bereft of ideals, without spiritual consciousness, living for material ends alone, and the very thought of it seized him with sickening horror. What a disgusting and dreadful hell this earth would be if it were populated by a race wholly destitute of faith in God! Struggle with doubt himself? Yes. But to bear on his conscience the guilt of infecting with that doubt the impressionable boys and girls in his own home, his classroom, his community? He could not be so inhuman, so cruel.

Asaph commands our admiration for another reason. Many a man, disillusioned about God, becomes cynical; he stops going to church, assumes the role of an agnostic, and flings away from religion altogether—which is a senseless thing to do, because he removes himself from those very spiritual resources which, in the end, might prove equal to his difficulties, bringing him through the mists of doubt into the bright sunlight of renewed faith. If Asaph felt tempted to become a cynic, his fine soul resisted the temptation. Wearied with the struggle, he did the wisest thing that any man can do. He turned to religion with a new earnestness, re-examined his beliefs with a new seriousness, went to church with a new humility, and as a result saw this obstacle in a new perspective. "But when I sought to understand this, it seemed to me a wearisome task, *until I went into the sanctuary of God* . . ." In the sanctuary of God—and that phrase may describe a building or it may describe a mind cleared of human prejudices and receptive to God's truth—certain great truths visited the Psalmist. If we ponder these truths, going beyond them to their implications, we may see that this obstacle to belief is not insuperable.

I

First, the Psalmist saw that *God is indeed just.* Outside in the world, in the hurly-burly of life where men think only in terms of human, materialistic values, it looked as though evil, far from being punished, paid off. Proud, violent, conceited, impious men enjoyed the reward promised to righteous people: prosperity, strength, peace in life and in death. But how different inside the sanctuary. There, in the atmosphere of eternal values, Asaph saw the prosperity of the wicked for what it really was — a house of cards vulnerable to every wind of circumstance.

> "then perceived I their end.
> Truly thou dost set them in slippery places;
>   thou dost make them fall to ruin.
> How they are destroyed in a moment,
>   swept away utterly by terrors!
> They are like a dream when one awakes,
>   on awakening you despise their phantoms."

This was no wishful thinking, because in Asaph's mind one truth now towered above all else. Evil, no matter how successful it appears in terms of wealth and power, is still evil at all times, in all places and in all people. Moreover, the moral order of God will have the last word on the evil-doer, and it will be a full answer given in God's own way and time. As Theodore Momsen wrote, "History has its nemesis for every sin." The evil-doer may be violent, conceited, powerful, but ultimately he must stand before that All-Powerful One who has commanded us to put faithfulness and righteousness above all else — and it will be a day of grim reckoning.

Why are we so anxious to establish the truth of God's justice, as though it were a comforting fact, one that worked out in our favour? Shakespeare said, "in the course of justice none of us should hope to see mercy"; and a Psalmist prayed that God would not enter into judgment with him, "for in thy sight shall no man living be justified". The truth that we seek here, far from being comfortable, may be the most

104

burning truth that we have ever known, one that we can no more endure than we can look directly at the light of the sun.

In his satire, *The Great Divorce*, C. S. Lewis takes us with a busload of ghosts who have made an excursion from hell to heaven with a view to remaining there permanently. There they meet the "solid people", the citizens of heaven; and one very Big Ghost is astonished to meet a man who on earth was tried and executed for murder. "What I'd like to understand," he explodes, "is what you're here for, as pleased as Punch, you, a murderer, while I've been walking the streets down there and living in a place like a pigsty all these years?" The solid person tries to explain that he has been forgiven, that both he and the man he murdered have been reunited at the judgment seat of God, but the Big Ghost is not having any of it. The injustice of the situation staggers him. "My rights!" he keeps shouting, "I've got to have my rights same as you, see." "Oh no," the solid person reassures him, "it's not as bad as all that. I haven't got my rights, or I should not be here. You will not get yours either. You will get something far better." But nothing placates the Big Ghost who angrily protests that he is not looking for mercy but for justice, and who stupidly does not realize that justice is exactly what he has received.

If we really want to establish the truth of God's justice, then we had better recognize that God is greater, sterner and more austere than our sentimental, popular Christianity commonly suggests. Our trouble is that we look for God only in the lovely, desirable, beautiful aspects of life, and seeing about us nothing but confusion and ugliness, we conclude that there cannot be a God or else that he is unjust. We forget that all of life comes under God's sovereignty, even the dark and distressing things, and that through these, if we listen carefully enough, the voice of God may be heard; indeed these may be the very manifestations of his justice. The men who wrote the Bible were realists. They found the presence of God and heard his voice speaking not only in sunshine but in storm, not only in the flower but in the earthquake, not only in plenty but in famine, not only in victory but in defeat. They saw the justice of God in life's sterner as well as its pleasanter aspects; they saw his relationship with them not in terms of comfort but in terms of power;

and it was never their fear that God would deal unjustly with them, but rather that he would be altogether too just.

"Why doesn't God do something?" Is that not the impatient cry of unspiritual men as they contemplate the tragedy of our world, the plight of refugees, the victories of Communism, the breakdown of diplomacy, the explosion of hydrogen bombs and the threat of nuclear war? Why doesn't God put a stop to it all? Why doesn't he do something? The answer may well be that through these tragedies God is judging us for our failure to respond to what he has already done. God put a world into our fumbling hands. He filled it with all that we could ask or think: forests of trees, green fields, flowing rivers, a wealth of coal and oil, gold and silver, arched by blue skies, rimmed with sunsets and rainbows. He filled his world with the possibility of miracles, the power of atoms, the strangeness of electricity, the wonder of sight and sound, taste and smell. He gave us the glory of the lighted mind, ordained to seek and find the secret power hidden in our universe. God set us on a high road with knowledge of good and evil, truth and error, right and wrong, guided by the miracle of conscience. At one very definite point in history God took the ultimate step, divested himself of heavenly glory, came where we are, showed us how to live, taught us the way of peace and freedom and happiness. All of this God has done for us, and if we step into the sanctuary long enough to think clearly, we shall not question God's justice any more; we shall prostrate ourselves before God in gratitude that he has not dealt with us more justly for defiling his world, desecrating his gifts, betraying his love and spurning the light which he has given us.

II

A second truth broke upon the Psalmist as he brooded over life in the sanctuary, the truth of *his own ignorance and blasphemy*. Like all devout Jews he believed the too-simple theory that God should reward righteousness and punish wickedness, but now for the first time he examined the implications of that theory. Suppose it worked? Suppose piety did automatically issue in prosperity and sin in suffering? Would that not deprive God of any independent judgment at all? Would it not make virtue prudential rather

106

than moral, and goodness a kind of celestial insurance policy taken out by shrewd, calculating, cold-blooded moralists for the sake of saving their own skins? The Psalmist did a very sane thing in the sanctuary: he forgot about the evil-doers and took a good look at himself. What of the wickedness of his own soul, the faithlessness, the blasphemy of exalting himself to the throne of the universe and usurping the sovereignty of Almighty God? Since when did God relegate to a mere man the right to decide just who is righteous and who is wicked, the right to administer Divine punishments and rewards? Asaph saw himself for what he was—a child petulantly upbraiding his father because the parent had not dispensed family discipline according to his childish conceptions of justice; worse than a child—an animal expecting from his master a piece of meat for his tricks and a kick for having fouled the household furniture. With shame the Psalmist poured out his confession:

> "When my soul was embittered,
>   when I was pricked in heart,
> I was stupid and ignorant,
>   I was like a beast toward thee."

Let us re-state the nature of this obstacle to Christian belief. We look about us and we see a world in moral chaos, a world where the good man gets the stick and the bad man gets the pie, where evil rides triumphant in the saddle while millions of innocent men suffer, and we say, "How can such a world possibly be governed by a good God?" But is that *all* we see in our world? What about certain other factors: the heroism and the devotion of Christian missionaries in hostile countries; the relief of human suffering now being administered by great national and international social agencies; the protest against racial and religious bigotry being offered by people who are able to think straightly and feel humanely; the championship of intellectual freedom and civil liberties by distinguished scientists, courageous educators and enlightened churchmen and laymen; the fresh, valiant, creative thinking which has been done and is being done with respect to the abolition of war and poverty; the faith, fidelity and devotion to be found in the best of our churches; the removal of historic barriers to fellowship in Christ; the emergence of a Church that is truly catholic in that it transcends divisions of nation, race and class. Before complaining about the injustice of God in our world situation, let us make certain that we look at the situation in its wholeness and take into account everything that God is doing. God, or someone like God, is doing marvellous things in our world today.

Asaph felt ashamed of himself for calling God's justice into account; it seemed almost beastly and unworthy of a man created in the image of God that he should hold such a constricted view of life and the universe. Perhaps, indeed, it is a form of pride, that selfish pride whereby we exalt ourselves to the centre of the universe and regard God as a cosmic nursemaid who exists only to make us comfortable. There is a more important truth than God's justice, the truth of God's total concern for the whole world of his creation, that order of God's providence in which saint and sinner alike live and move and have their being. Whether we approve the Divine discipline or not, this world is still the Father's house, and if we could get ourselves out of the picture just long enough to focus our faith on the larger canvas, we should realize that God has a greater purpose to fulfil and a greater wisdom to fulfil it than we are capable of imagining. Such a vision came to Asaph in the sanctuary, as it will come to us.

III

In the quiet of the sanctuary Asaph learned another truth: he learned that goodness finds its reward not in any favours that God confers but in something more marvellous, *the giving of God himself*.

> "Nevertheless I am continually with thee;
>   thou dost hold my right hand.
> Thou dost guide me with thy counsel,
>   and afterward thou wilt receive me to glory."

There is something worse in life than having to suffer innocently, and that is the feeling that you have to suffer alone. Imagine a child lying desperately ill in a garret, lonely, unloved and uncared for; nothing could be more hideously chill and depressing. Now imagine a mother present, bending over the child, entering into its suffering, surrounding it with an atmosphere of love. There is no less pain, no less poverty, yet the mother's loving companionship makes the whole grim situation so infinitely more tolerable. The worst thing about atheism is not that it leads to badness but that it leads to an incurable sadness and loneliness. The religious man may not suffer less for being religious, but neither does he suffer alone. Beside him is a Presence, One who cares for him intimately, enters into all the feeling of his infirmities and surrounds him with an atmosphere of love.

There is something worse in life than helplessness in the presence of evil forces, and that is that we should be helpless abstractly and absolutely. "No God!" declares the atheist. We can only reply, "What, then, do you offer us in place of God?" To renounce our faith does not improve the situation, but only makes it worse, only leaves us to our own frail human resources at the mercy of a vast, unconscious, immoral machine. The religious man may be no less helpless for being religious, but at least he is not helpless in a vacuum; he has a source of stability, a strength that undergirds him, something older and greater than himself to which he can cling.

There is something worse in life than confusion on the world scene, and that is that we should have no idea of how to live in the midst of confusion. The German philosopher, Nietzsche, was one of the few men in history who, having rejected God, faced the consequences of his decision. He knew that the denial of God meant the denial of all moral values, the denial of any real sense of direction, and he carried his "sad lantern" down all the corridors of human life and finally completed the syllogism of his logic by going mad. The religious man may have no less confusion around him for being religious, but at least he himself is not confused; his life moves with a sense of high purpose and he feels himself impelled in the direction of goals that are worthwhile.

There is something worse in life than the darkness of doubt and despair, and that is that we should be unable to see beyond the darkness. Two travellers crossing a frozen pond at night: one of them slips on the ice, falls, hurts himself, curses the darkness and exclaims, "What's the use?"; the other slips and falls, but because he can see a light on the far shore he gets up and struggles on, knowing that love and warmth await him at the end of the journey. The religious man will not have an easier life for being religious—a more difficult life, perhaps, because religion brings him into closer touch with reality; but it will never be a life of unrelieved despair, because he lives it in the eternal perspective and because through all the darkness of the journey he can see the light of home.

To be sure, belief in a good God comes hard when the terrible injustices of life beat like destroying winds on our souls, and we are tempted to fling away from the faith altogether; but shall we fling away from our only source of companionship, support, guidance and hope? Shall we do this and still live? That truth broke upon the Psalmist as he struggled with his doubts in the sanctuary. In that dark hour he nearly became an atheist; but in that dark hour he realized also that when a man loses God he has lost everything, he has nothing left.

10

Unanswered Prayer

THE late Maude Royden, who preached in the City Temple for two years during the First World War, told of a soldier who returned home after fighting with the British Forces. His rejoicing family said that they knew that he would come back unharmed because they had prayed for him. "Don't talk like that!" he protested, "I cannot bear it! It is just chance who comes back and who dies. I prayed for people in the war who have been killed!" Then he told them a tragic story. He had been watching some men retreating under enemy fire. Running as fast as they could, the men reached a little thicket where they took cover. There was just a possibility that some of them might be saved. Then the scrub caught fire and the men were burned to death. The young soldier who told the story said that he and his friends had to sit and watch them. They prayed in their anguish that God would extricate their comrades. "We said to God, 'For mercy's sake do something for these men. If they must die, let them die quickly. Let them be put out of their agony.' But no answer came. The heavens were as brass." He added bitterly, "What is the use of telling me that you have protected me by your prayers? How could we have been protected when the other men were left to burn to death? We prayed with passion, with madness, and we were not heard."

Here is a forbidding obstacle to Christian /belief—the perplexing problem of unanswered prayer. If you have tried the Christian experiment and done any praying at all, then you have not only thought about it but actually known the discouraging and frustrating experience of pouring out your soul's petition to a dull, unanswering silence. Through circumstances beyond your control you found yourself trapped in some intolerable situation with not a glimmer of light to penetrate the darkness. Each day the burden of it weighed more heavily on you and you wondered how much longer you could go on. A pious friend said, "Why don't you pray about it?" "Pray!" you retorted bitterly, "I have been on my knees every day for months, but what good has it done? Things don't get better; they get worse. God is not listening to me. I am not sure any more that there is a God!"

On such occasions the Bible can be more irritating than helpful. The Bible is full of unanswered prayers. Moses prays to enter the Promised Land but dies on a mountain-top, his request refused. The Psalmist sobs out his cry of dereliction, "My God, my God, why hast thou forsaken me? Why art thou so far from helping me, and from the words of my complaint?" Habakkuk in his despondency exclaims, "O Lord, how long shall I cry and thou wilt not hear?" Paul prays three times that a vexatious physical handicap, a "thorn in his flesh", "a sharp pain", as *The New English Bible* translates it, which hinders his missionary labours, may be removed, but he is compelled to make the best of it and to let it make the best of him. "Three times I besought the Lord about this that it should leave me, but . . ." It has been suggested that the rest of Paul's biography, written in the fashion of twentieth-century Christianity, would run like this: "After these things, Paul began to lose interest and fell away from the Church . . . His thorn was there to stay; obviously prayer could not budge it. He read some books on prayer; still it did not seem to work. Perhaps he could get along just as well without praying. Why not? He went back to his trade and made tents. He amassed quite a fortune for those days — before he died. The years grew very tranquil and undisturbed in their slow and equal pace from day to day. It was a great relief to be rid of all the wearing obligations of religion, except, of course, that he was never quite happy."

In attempting to scale this barrier of unanswered prayer, perhaps we should recognize at the outset that the major part of our praying does not require an answer at all. There was a wealthy gentleman who became rather bitter about his sons and daughters because, as he said, "The only time I ever hear from them is when they want something. Why don't they come to see me just for my own sake?" I am sure that God feels the same way towards us at times. It must insult the Almighty God that we cast him in the role of a celestial chore boy loafing around his universe pitifully pleading to be made use of. Study the prayers of the saints.

Rarely do they ask God for anything save the clearer knowledge of his will. The great men of prayer seem content simply to dwell in God's presence, to reflect upon the wonder and the mystery of his being, and to worship and adore him because he is God and they are men. Were God never to grant us another favour in our lives, words still could not exhaust our indebtedness for what he has already done, his gifts in creating us, in providing for our daily needs, in redeeming us with the precious blood of Christ. Leslie Weatherhead has written a helpful manual of private devotion in which he construes prayer as a house with seven rooms: the rooms of *affirmation, thanksgiving, confession, reception, petition, intercession,* and *meditation.* How pitifully restricted we should be if our entire spiritual life were lived in just one or two rooms of this large and varied mansion. Even though we never ask favours of God, we can still enjoy a full-orbed relationship with him. So much of the soul's communion with God requires no answer from him at all.

At the same time we ought not to leave unused those two rooms of petition and intercession—prayers that voice our own needs and the needs of those dearest to us in faith that God will answer them. The elderly gentleman may resent his sponging children, but he would feel equally hurt if they failed to call upon him in a time of trouble. So God, who cares for us with a Father's love, stands by ready to help us with a Father's help, and he longs to hear us say that we still need him. In his own Word God urges us to pray confidently: "Call unto me and I will answer thee . . . Ask, and it shall be given you . . . If ye shall ask anything in my name, I will do it . . . The effectual, fervent prayer of a righteous man availeth much." Great and precious promises, they awaken such expectation in our hearts; but the question we are asking now is, Can we believe them? The plain truth is that God has not always kept these promises. We have prayed, we have prayed with passion, with madness, and we were not heard.

In his little devotional book, *The Meaning of Prayer,* Harry Emerson Fosdick includes a masterly chapter, to which I am indebted, in which he comes to grips with this thorny problem of the religious life. He suggests some possible reasons why our prayers may seem to go unanswered. One reason certainly is the ignorance of our asking. As Paul wrote

113

in his Roman Letter, "we do not know how to pray as we ought". The Bible tells us that when King Solomon ascended the throne of his father, David, God appeared to him in a dream and offered to grant any favour that Solomon might wish: long life, riches, or victory in battle. To his everlasting credit the young king waved these worldly advantages aside and instead asked God for a wise and discerning mind to govern his people righteously. The choice so pleased God that he granted Solomon not only the gift of wisdom, but these other gifts as well. Because the young king had sought first the Kingdom of God and his righteousness, these other things were added unto him. But all men do not have the innate wisdom of Solomon in their dealings with God. Sometimes we pray intelligently; but sometimes we offer petitions which in themselves are quite impossible of fulfilment and which, if God did fulfil them, would turn out to our detriment instead of our well-being. The poet Longfellow has said, "What discord we should bring into the universe if all our prayers were answered! Then we should govern the world and not God. And do you think we should govern it better? It gives me pain to hear the long, wearisome petitions of men asking for they know not what."

God is not unaware of our needs; in fact, he knows them better than we know them. When Jesus related his parable about the friend at midnight who crawled out of bed at a late hour to help a troublesome neighbour, he was trying to show us that the very needs of our lives speak more eloquently to God than any words we can use to describe them. F. W. Norwood told of a pious young preacher in Australia who called on a farmer during a prolonged drought, a man whose ranch was fairly burning up under the blistering sun. He suggested to the ranchman that they pray together for rain. "Come over here," said the ranchman, "and listen." They went over to the side of the house and there heard the sound of sheep dying of thirst, "Ugh! Ugh!" — like a man coughing. "Can you pray like that?" asked the ranchman. "And if you can, will the God who does not answer their prayer answer yours?"

God does not listen to our words; he listens to the groanings which cannot be uttered, and it is these that he answers, not necessarily our expressed desires. Jesus taught us to think of God as a Father. Take human fatherhood at its best, he said, its kindest, most generous, most loving best, and you have only *begun* to understand the true nature of God. The greatest of all prayers Jesus climaxed by saying, "If ye, then, being evil, know how to give good gifts to your children, how much more shall your heavenly Father give good things to them that ask him?" But you fathers, do you give your children everything they ask for? Do you not say "No" occasionally, denying immediate requests when these conflict with your larger purpose for the development of personality and the growth of character? Of course, the youngsters do not always see it that way. It does not make sense to them that they should be denied money or clothing or other privileges in order that they develop in the hard way a mature and realistic scale of values. But it makes sense to you. However much you hate to do it, you have to say "No" to your child sometimes simply because you love him. Sometimes God says "No" too, says it because he loves us, because he knows what is good for us better than we know ourselves. Sometimes God turns what seems a deaf ear to our expressed petitions in order to answer what he knows to be our deepest needs.

Dr. Fosdick recalls that passage from Augustine's *Confessions* where he pictures his mother praying all one night that God would not let her son sail for Italy. She wanted Augustine to be a Christian, and she could not endure seeing him pass from her influence. If under her care he was still far from being Christ's, what would he be amid the licentiousness and splendour and alluring temptations of Italy? But even while she prayed passionately for her son's retention at home, he sailed by the grace of God for Italy where, persuaded by Ambrose, he became a Christian in the very place from which his mother's prayers would have kept him. Her petition was denied, but the need of her son was granted. God knew what was good for her and for her son better than she knew herself. Augustine gave thanks to God: "Thou in the depth of thy counsels, hearing the main point of her desire, regarded not what she then asked that thou mightest make me what she ever desired." Thus it is possible that God says "No" to some of our petitions because of the ignorance of our asking.

It may be that some of our prayers go unanswered because we pray continually for the things that we are intended to

115

achieve by ourselves. We must not make prayer a substitute for intelligence and hard work. Consider, indeed, what an undisciplined, effortless, stagnant sort of world this would become if everything could be accomplished simply by praying for it. If, as in fairy tales, we had the power of omnipotent wishing conferred upon us, we should never use our intelligence at all. If life is to mean development and discipline, then there are some petitions which God will not grant, no matter how fervently we offer them. When a boy asks his father to do his homework because he wishes to play, will the father—assuming that he is equal to his son's homework—do it? Not if he loves the lad and cares for his growth of character. The father, in answer to the boy's request, may encourage him, assist him, stand by him and see him through, but he must not do for his son anything that the boy can possibly do for himself. Harsh though it may seem, God must surely require us as individuals and as a race to endure the discipline of painful enterprise and struggle rather than find an easy relief by prayer.

Now, I believe that God does answer prayer, and answers it in ways more marvellous than we can ever imagine. Why not? Scripture throbs with a single theme—the competence of God. "Now unto him who is able to do exceeding abundantly above all that we ask or think . . ." That which lies beyond our control does not lie beyond his control; that which is impossible to us is not impossible to him. Think of Eddie Rickenbacker's simple, direct account of his little group of airmen forced down in the Pacific during the war and adrift on their rubber rafts for several days. One man had a New Testament and was reading it. That struck Eddie Rickenbacker as a good idea, so each morning and evening they joined the rafts in a rough triangle, and in turn the men read passages of Scripture and joined in the Lord's Prayer. Some became backsliders when the prayers did not seem to be answered at once, but others persisted. Then deliverance came. When they were starving a seagull lit on Eddie's hat, and they had food. When they were dying of thirst, a passing shower drenched them. When they were too weak to pull the last few hundred yards to land, superhuman strength seemed to be given them. No wonder that their first act upon reaching shore was to kneel down and thank God for their deliverance.

Eddie Rickenbacker and his comrades had a right to pray. What else could they do under the circumstances? Helpless themselves and cut off from all human assistance, they were so at the mercy of the elements that nothing but an act of God could bring them to safety. Only in such extremity, only when we have exhausted all our own resources, have we a right to look up to heaven and ask God for a miracle. Prayer is not magic, even though some people persistently behave as if it were. Prayer is not asking God to do for us what we should be doing for ourselves. Prayer is putting the best we have at God's disposal, our best brains and our hardest work, offering them to him as channels of his grace and power. Perhaps we have no business praying at all until we have done our best to create the conditions under which our prayer can be answered: no business praying for physical health until we have seen a doctor; no business praying about our teeth until we have been to a dentist; no business praying about our emotional problems until we have had a talk with a psychiatrist; no business praying for spiritual growth until we have prefaced it with an honest effort to discipline ourselves in the Christian life; no business praying for social justice and world peace until greed, lust, hatred, acquisitiveness and all other tempers that provoke strife have been exorcised from our own hearts. Let us be guided by this prayer of the late W. E. Orchard: "O God, forgive the poverty, the pettiness, the childish folly of our prayers. Listen not to our words but to the groanings that cannot be uttered; hearken not to our petitions but to the crying of our need. So often we pray for that which is already ours, neglected and unappropriated; so often for that which can never be ours; so often for that which we must win ourselves, and then labour endlessly for that which can only come to us in prayer."

Perhaps our prayers go unanswered because of our unreadiness to receive an answer. Notice how often the New Testament conjoins the word "prayer" with the word "faith" or "believe". "Ask in faith, nothing wavering . . . Whatsoever things ye desire, when ye pray, believe that ye shall receive them, and ye shall have them." Can that be the source of our difficulty—our lack of faith, our unreceptiveness to God, our unreadiness to receive an answer from him? We pray, but with tongue in cheek; we do not seriously believe that

God will answer our prayers; we might die of heart failure if he ever did.

H. G. Wells wrote a satirical short story about an Archbishop perplexed by his own state of mind. His nerve, which had never failed him before, was failing him now, and he felt desperate about it. He had always been a man who had kept his own counsel, but now, if only he could find understanding, sympathy, endorsement. If anyone else had come to him in this sort of predicament, he would have said softly in that rich, kind voice of his, "Try prayer, my son, try prayer." Why not himself try prayer? It came to him that he had not made a particular and personal appeal to God on his own behalf for many years. It had seemed unnecessary. He had, of course, said his prayers with the utmost regularity. Prayer he had regarded as a purifying, beneficial process, no more to be neglected than brushing his teeth. But a sense of a Hearer listening at the other end of a telephone, so to speak, behind the veil, had always been a faint one. In this particular tangle, however, the Archbishop wanted something more definite. Yes, he would pray; in his own private chapel he would pray. Slowly he sank to his knees and put his hands together. "O God," he began, and paused. He paused, and a sense of awful imminence, a monstrous awe gripped him. He heard a voice, not a harsh voice, but a clear, strong voice, neither friendly nor hostile. "Yes," said the voice. "What is it?" They found His Grace in the morning. He had slipped off the steps on which he had been kneeling and lay sprawling on the crimson carpet. Plainly his death had been instantaneous.

We give up too easily in our prayers. We are not serious enough, not insistent enough, not patient enough in our praying. In the early years of my ministry I had a mortal dread of calling on strangers in their homes. I would go to the front door of a house, ring the bell once, and if no one came, breathe a sigh of relief, leave my card, and walk away quickly; whereas if I had been more bold, I should have waited on the doorstep and rung the bell several times. We have that kind of timidity in our praying. We give up too easily. Jesus taught us to pray without ceasing. "He spake a parable unto them to the end that they ought always to pray and not to faint," and the parable recorded a woman's tiresome, reiterated petitioning of a judge so that finally out of sheer exasperation he dealt with her case. Remember, that in this parable the judge stands in contrast with God, not in similarity with him, and the lesson is: If it was worthwhile waiting patiently upon the unjust judge, how much more surely worthwhile to wait patiently on the Fatherly God. "Yes" and "No" are not the only answers to prayer. God continually gives us another answer—"Wait!" Spurgeon put the case strongly: "It may be your prayer is like a ship which does not come home for a long time, but when it does come home it has richer freight. Mere 'coasters' will bring you coals, or such like, ordinary things; but they that go afar to Tarshish return with gold and ivory. Coasting prayers, such as we pray every day, bring us many necessaries, but there are great prayers which, like the old Spanish galleons, cross the main ocean and are longer out of sight, but come home deep-laden with a golden freight." We need to be more persistent in prayer. Some things God cannot give us until we are ready for them. Prayer as a spiritual discipline makes us ready. Prayer cleans the house, washes the windows, hangs the curtains, sets the table, opens the door, until God says, "Now, the house is in order. The guest may come in."

The ignorance of our petition, our use of prayer where it does not belong, our unreadiness to receive an answer—surely these factors throw some light on the problem of unanswered prayer. But is there such a thing as *unanswered* prayer if we keep our lives in harmony with God? Dr. Fosdick makes bold to say that God always answers prayer in one of two ways: either he changes the circumstances or he supplies sufficient power to overcome them; he answers either the petition or the man. Come back to the Apostle Paul. We know how God really completed the story of that man's life. "Three times I besought the Lord about this that it should leave me, but he said to me, 'My grace is sufficient for you, for my power is made perfect in weakness.'" God did not make life easier for Paul, but he did give the apostle strength for life's demands. He did not remove the nagging thorn in his flesh, but he did help him to live with the thorn and transform it into a means of Divine grace. God did not answer Paul's petition, but he did answer Paul himself.

Does it not help immeasurably to remember that Christ our Lord experienced in Gethsemane what we call unanswered prayer? Look upon that kneeling figure, so majestic in grief and so wonderful in woe. "Father, all things are possible unto thee. Take this cup away from me." All the world's anguish filled that bitter cup—pain of body, mind and spirit. You have never imagined what prayer can be like until you have heard the Son of God pounding on the door of heaven and watched him wrestling in a bloody sweat with the inscrutable will of his Father. Suppose the Master's petition had been answered and the Cross miraculously removed from his path? Where should we be now? Where would be the good news of man's salvation, the victory over sin and death, the hope of everlasting blessedness? God meets the need of the world through the unanswered prayer of Christ. How well the Master knew it! Quickly he turned from his own natural desire to pray that God's will might be done through him: "Yet not what I will but what thou wilt." And that deeper prayer God answered more gloriously than tongue or pen can show. God always answers prayer when we keep our lives in harmony with his will. If he happens to refuse our specific requests, it may be just his way of saying that he is going to take over, going to stride beyond our little horizons as though they did not exist and write such a fulfilment to our lives as we have never dreamed of. But whatever God's answer, our prayer will bring, as it brought to Paul and to our Lord himself, guidance, support, companionship, the assurance of God's all-sufficient grace.

II

The Absence of Religious Experience

"IF I ONLY had your experience in the Christian life; if
I possessed your sense of certainty about spiritual things;
if I could pray as you do and be sure that Someone out there
is actually listening to me; if I could go to Church and take
the Sacrament and come away, just as you do, feeling
refreshed and strengthened; if I could have the faith that
releases radiance and power in your life and in the lives of
other convinced Christians; if I could actually experience
the love of God and the Saviourhood of Christ and the
guidance of the Holy Spirit, just as you have experienced
them — then I should be a Christian. But none of these things
have happened to me. I feel like a blind man in a dark room
looking for a black cat that isn't there."

Here, then, is another obstacle to Christian belief — the
absence of any specific, positive, definable religious experience. In attempting to scale it, we must be very clear what
we mean by a religious experience and we must understand
at the outset that we may be looking for something that
simply does not exist.

There is no such thing as a stereotyped religious experience. In the Federal Bureau of Investigation Building in
Washington they have on file the fingerprints of millions of
American citizens, and the experts tell us that among all these
millions no two fingerprints are exactly alike. As human
beings differ in their physical characteristics, so do they
differ in their experience of God. William James wrote a
famous book called *The Varieties of Religious Experience* which,
as the title implies, leads us to believe that if we want to
know how many varieties there are, then we must count
the number of human beings who have lived on this planet
in all the millenniums since man first became conscious of
God. The writers of the New Testament came into touch
with one and the same Christ, but how different are their
portraits of him. Obviously Christ means to John something

different than he does to Luke, and to Paul something different than he means to Mark. Read Augustine's *Confessions*, or Thomas à Kempis's *Imitation of Christ* or John Wesley's *Grace Abounding*. These writings grow out of an authentic and profound experience of the same Christ, the same salvation, the same destiny, but an experience so richly diverse in its effect and its interpretation.

No man should count it an obstacle to Christian belief that he has not come to know God in precisely the same way as the next man. Vital religion has a quality of sacred intimacy like the love of a husband and wife. The inner substance of a man's faith is something that he can neither describe nor impart, and even to make the attempt would seem a sacrilege. Only in its outward form does his relationship with God conform to a general pattern and possess those basic elements of religious experience upon which any man can lay hold and make his own and through which he can come to a direct, first-hand, saving knowledge of God in Jesus Christ. We see this pattern in the Bible and in the lives of saintly men who walked in comradeship with God and to whom God was as real as the stars in the heavens and the leaves on the trees. It will help us in confronting this obstacle to look specifically at one man, the prophet Isaiah who in his early life had an experience of God so dramatic and vivid that it impelled and sustained him throughout his entire career. What happened to him in the temple seems almost like a symphony in its four rhythmic movements, or like the swing of a pendulum moving between God and man.

I

First, there is *a dramatic vision of God*. The pendulum swings from God to man. It is God who takes the initiative and moves into the life of his servant with a Divine act of grace and power. Let us ponder this truth, because so often we take the initiative ourselves and we go searching for God as if he were a fickle butterfly flitting from one flower to another and eluding our grasp. "I took a day to search for God," sings the poet. "And found him not," he adds. We shall never find God by reaching up to heaven and seeking him through reasoned argument and mystic contemplation. We shall never find God at all; rather we shall be found by him, as God in his love for us reaches down from heaven and moves into our lives with grace and power. This is always the first element in religious experience.

"But," you protest, "this is precisely what has never happened to me. I know it has happened to the saints and to many convinced Christian people, but I cannot recall any specific instance where a sense of the supernatural has invaded my world." Can you not? There is a delightful touch in the make-believe story a small boy once told his father. "We were all going down the street, when suddenly along comes God." Surely most of us can recall days when something came along, something from beyond the world o time and sense, some influence or power not our own that penetrated our earthly experience like a shaft of sunlight breaking through the clouds. As Robert Browning saw it, "Along comes God" into the drab lives of bewildered people through the Song of Pippa, the silk winder's daughter, whose passing made all things different. William Wordsworth understood that "along comes God" by Tintern Abbey in "a presence that disturbed him with the joy of elevated thoughts". I read of a window cleaner on the Empire State Building in New York who looked out from the one-hundred-and-second floor and said that as he saw the storm below and the bright sunlight above he felt the reality of God. We have all felt that reality—in a moment of ecstatic joy or in an hour of deep sorrow, in the handclasp of a friend or the laughter of a child, in an impulse to generosity that took us unawares, or a twinge of conscience that broke through our defences and compelled us to be honest with ourselves.

"Along comes God" to Isaiah in the temple. This young man of noble birth entered the sacred place in a profoundly serious mood, because the king had just died, bringing to an end a whole era in the life of the nation Israel. The bubble of false security and prosperity had burst, and Israel now saw herself a pathetically small, unprotected state wedged between the two empires, Egypt and Assyria, and about to be sucked into the whirlpool of struggle for world power. Their fools' paradise had come to an end, and fear gripped the hearts of the people. Isaiah had always believed in God, but now as he entered the temple to pray for Divine guidance and strength in this time of national crisis, suddenly a vision of

God's majesty and holiness broke upon him. He describes it in language which has become very precious:

"In the year that King Uzziah died I saw also the Lord sitting upon the throne, high and lifted up, and his train filled the temple. Above it stood the seraphims: each one had six wings; with twain he covered his face, and with twain he covered his feet, and with twain he did fly. And one cried unto another, and said, Holy, holy, holy, is the Lord of hosts: the whole earth is full of his glory. And the posts of the door moved at the voice of him who cried, and the house was filled with smoke."

The details of this unusual event do not matter. What does matter is that in a moment of deep significance God took the initiative and moved into the life of his servant with irresistible grace and power. Religious experience begins there —with God taking the initiative. How much clearer this becomes in the New Testament where we see Jesus, the love of God in action, invading the lives of people when they least expect it. To Peter beside the Sea of Galilee he says, "Put out into the deep and let down your nets for a catch." To Zacchaeus up the sycamore tree he calls, "Make haste and come down, for today I must abide at thy house." Of a hardened adulteress by Jacob's Well he asks a favour, "Give me water to drink." To Saul on the Damascus Road he comes in a dazzling light and a voice from the unseen, "Saul, Saul, why persecutest thou me?" Always he takes the initiative. Men do not find him; rather they are found by him, sometimes in spite of themselves, and having been found, they know that the unseen and eternal God has come within the orbit of their lives.

Let no man say that he has never seen a vision of God. It needs no mystic exultation, no shivers up the spine to convince us that God has taken the initiative and laid hold upon us with grace and power. We have only to stand with Isaiah in the accustomed place of worship where Bible and Sacrament remind us unceasingly of a story old but ever new, the living and dying of the Lord Jesus. In Graham Greene's novel, *The Heart of the Matter*, the English chief of police in an African colony, whose life has become involved in a tangled web of intrigue, adultery and murder, lunges toward the brink of suicide; but before taking his life he goes to church, more to curse God than to pray. There before the altar he fastens his gaze upon the Cross and he feels that eternal love of God which has once and for all thrust itself into a situation that hates and defies him. "How desperately God must love me," he cries. That is the first element in religious experience and we can make it our own — the vision of what God has done for us because he loves us.

II

The second element in a religious experience is *the confession of sin*. The pendulum has swung from God to man; now it swings back again in man's response. And such a response! "Woe is me! for I am undone; because I am a man of unclean lips, and I dwell in the midst of a people of unclean lips: for mine eyes have seen the King, the Lord of hosts." This is no morbid admission of guilt, no self-induced penitence, no whining and cajoling before the presence of the Most High in the hope of gaining Divine favour. This is the innermost nature of man's sinfulness clearly revealed in the awful light of God's purity. Set anything imperfect against the background of something perfect, and its blemishes will stand out in stark hideousness. Shakespeare's Iago said of Cassio, "He hath a daily beauty that makes me ugly." Men felt that way in the presence of Jesus, and that is why wicked men wished him out of their sight. It is always true that the closer we draw to God, the more conscious we become of our own sin. From the vision of God's holiness Isaiah could only turn his gaze upon himself and upon the world about him and cry out in penitent despair, "Woe is me! for I am undone; because I am a man of unclean lips, and I dwell in the midst of a people of unclean lips."

Every now and then some particularly vapid social scientist attacks the Church's emphasis on sin as "a psychopathic aspect of adolescent mentality". "The true function of religion," he claims, "is not to drag men down but to build them up, not to stultify their personalities, but rather to help them become healthy, enlightened and mature." A discerning criticism, because the attempt in human language to convince people that they are miserable sinners is not only despicable but downright impossible. No parent ever improved a child's character by shouting at him, "You are a naughty boy!"; nor did any evangelist ever save souls merely by whipping up a sense of guilt in his hearers. We know the

125

poverty of our lives, our emptiness, our futility, our enslavement to selfish and destructive passion; and we know the predicament of our world, the blind, materialistic forces that sweep us headlong from one catastrophe to another. As Walter Lippmann has said, "Even with the best will in the world, the unregenerate man can only muddle into muddle." Still we remain proud, however. We rationalize our sin, we psychologize about it, we refuse to face it, until suddenly God moves into our lives with such a vision of his holiness that we cannot escape his blinding light, and in his presence we know ourselves judged. We see that vision in the Cross where God in Christ has acted dramatically and decisively to save us from our sins. We see how seriously God treats our sins and how ultimate and terrible is the price that he pays to forgive them. Human denunciations may simply irritate us and harden us in our obstinate pride, but before the Cross, God's act of grace and power, we know ourselves to be men of unclean lips who dwell in the midst of a people of unclean lips, because our eyes have seen the King, the Lord of hosts.

A minister was asked by a lady in his congregation to visit her sick brother, a man who had squandered the major part of his rather aimless life in Mexico, had lost most of his money, had contracted a serious illness, and now sullen and bitter and determined to die had thrown himself on the mercy of his widowed sister. Confined to his bed, he refused to see anyone, even a doctor, so you can imagine his anger when this total stranger entered his room. However, the stranger remained a stranger, and with his discreet, sympathetic approach, managed to draw some measure of response from the poor fellow. The response, in fact, was beyond expectation, because a second visit was encouraged, and a third, until the bonds of understanding began to form. One day the minister related a story, a simple story about a foolish boy who left his father's house, went into a far country, squandered his money, fell into evil ways, crawled the gutter of humiliation, came to his senses, and returned home to be welcomed and forgiven by his father. After the minister had finished speaking, the man looked at him and said, "What's that story got to do with me?" "That," came the reply, "is how God deals with a sinner who is sorry for his sins." "Who are you, anyway?" asked the sick man. "I am a minister, your sister's minister." There was a moment of silence, then a burst of racking sobs, scalding tears of shame and remorse over a life utterly wasted. But the shackles had been broken, the crucial step taken, and from that moment the fires of hope began to burn. That is the second element in religious experience and we can make that our own—a humble confession of sin.

III

The third element is *the sense of being forgiven*. The pendulum, which has swung in repentance from man to God, now swings back to man with God's forgiveness.

"Then flew one of the seraphims unto me, having a live coal in his hand, which he had taken with the tongs from off the altar; And he laid it upon my mouth, and said, Lo, this hath touched thy lips; and thine iniquity is taken away, and thy sin is purged."

We must grasp the completeness of this operation. There is nothing provisional about it, no strings attached, no moral stipulations, as though to say, "Yes, I know you are a sinful man, but you have admitted it now, so there is hope for you. Take hold of yourself. Reform your conduct. Try to lead a better life, and one of these days we shall talk the whole matter over again." None of that. When God forgives a man, he forgives him unreservedly. As Dwight L. Moody said, "God has put our sins not only where we cannot see them; he has put them where *he* cannot see them." God grants more than we bargain for when we ask his forgiveness; he demands no explanations, no recital of extenuating circumstances, no promise of restitution. God takes a sinner exactly as he is, accepts him in the midst of his sin and in spite of his sin, and restores that sinner to fellowship with himself.

I could scarcely believe the change which had taken place in a young man I had known a decade earlier as a rather dissipated person, frivolous, self-centred, and altogether indifferent toward the Church and religion. His one interest in those days was keeping up with a rather fast crowd in the theatre. Now I saw him teaching a class of boys in the Sunday School and moving about with a new buoyancy in his step and a new light in his eyes. It was obvious that he wanted to talk to me; he seemed bursting to tell me something. At last,

127

when we were alone, I asked him, "What has happened to you? You are changed. Apart from being ten years older you actually look ten years younger, like a man who has taken a six-months rest cure." "Something more wonderful than that," he burst out. "Since you last saw me I have had a religious experience. It came upon me so unexpectedly. One afternoon I was sitting alone in the house and I felt the presence of God right beside me. I could almost have reached out and touched him. But what did God want with me? The whole picture of my wasted life flashed before my eyes, and I couldn't hold back the tears. I must have sat there most of the afternoon, just feeling ashamed, with my head buried in my hands. But then, I began to feel a strange sense of peace, just as though everything was going to be all right; the past did not matter any more, only the future mattered. I became a new man that afternoon."

The forgiveness of God is radical, just like that. When his love possesses our lives, it does not merely cleanse and recondition them, it does not merely heal them like surgery, clearing away the cancerous tissues and restoring our spiritual soundness, so that we can take up the same life again with renewed health and strength. God's forgiving grace is far more drastic than that; it makes an end of us as the people we are, it kills us, buries us, and erases our names from the book of life; then it resurrects us as new creatures with new names, new personalities who need not be ashamed of our past because we have no past to convict us. "If any man be in Christ," wrote Paul, "he is a new creature; old things are passed away; behold all things are become new." This is the third element in religious experience and we can make this our own — the sense of God's forgiveness; and it comes to the man who, acknowledging his sin in the light of God's holiness, surrenders his pride and turns to God with sorrow and repentance.

IV

Already we have anticipated the final element in a vital religious experience — *an act of commitment to God*. Having swung from God to man, then back to God and back again to man, the pendulum must now swing once more from man to God. Suddenly the young Isaiah, shaken out of his mystic trance, remembers the fearful human situation that exists outside the temple. God's people in their proud, materialistic extravagance are skidding down a slippery slope to their own doom. Someone must warn them. Someone must recall them from this apostasy back to their ancient covenant with God. Someone must be God's prophet to them. It will not be a pleasant task, for men like to be cheered and soothed; they do not welcome the spokesman for God who confronts them with their waywardness, forces them to face their sins, summons them to repentance and threatens them with Divine punishment if they fail. "Whom shall I send, and who will go for us?" Isaiah has been waiting for these words, knowing that it now lies within his power either to seal or cancel this profound religious experience. The next move is up to him. He must say "Yes" to God. So he gives the only reply, "Here am I; send me."

With so many people religious experience breaks down at exactly that point. They pass readily through the first three stages—the revelation of God in Christ, the confession of sin, the acceptance of God's forgiveness; but when it comes to this final, decisive stage of surrender, commitment, consecration, their nerve fails, and they look longingly at the shackles on their wrists and decide that slavery, though not preferable, at least offers more security than freedom. Churches are full of people who have never experienced a first-hand, saving knowledge of God in Jesus Christ. They have been listening to the Gospel all their lives, but they have never made it their own as a redeeming power. They are religious by hearsay rather than by vital apprehension and insight. Someone has called them "second-hand Christians". The fault lies not in their minds; they know the truth about God in Christ and they partly believe it. Nor in their hearts; they may not care for high-flown theories of sin and salvation, but they know the poverty of their own lives and in their souls they want to be right again with God. The fault lies in their wills, the centre of action and decision; it lies in their reluctance to break loose, their unreadiness to take a venture of faith, their refusal to say "yes" to God, their unwillingness to put their lives into the hands of Christ so that, like a potter, he may shatter them and remould them according to his own designs.

There *are* such things as "barriers to belief", practical and

theoretical obstacles that prevent us from moving forward
to a whole-hearted acceptance of the Christian Faith. With
most people, however, the big barrier lies within themselves.
In plain truth they do not want to believe the Christian Faith,
because deep down they know what that belief might involve, and they are not willing to pay the price. They are
afraid to hear the words, "Whom shall I send, and who will
go for us?", afraid because they are not prepared to answer,
"Here am I, send me." We need not envy the religious
experience of other people. We can make our own religious
experience, if we are willing to take the steps needed to
acquire it. This obstacle can be scaled very simply. To have
the Christian experience you must make the Christian
experiment. There may indeed be much about Christianity
that you cannot accept, much about God that you cannot
understand, but of this you can be sure: God wants you;
he calls you to a life in friendship with him, a life on his terms
and in his service, and he longs to hear you say "Yes".

12

Hypocrisy in the Church

A LONDON newspaper, the *Sunday Pictorial*, carried an important series of articles about the Church and Christianity. The writer, Norman Price, found himself challenged by his two sons, ages six and nineteen, to prove the reality of God in a world where everything seems to deny that reality. So Norman Price began a search for God, for his two boys, and in the series of articles he tells where the search led him. First he consulted the "experts". He wrote to half a dozen Bishops, outlining his problem and promising that their replies would be read by fifteen million people. What a colossal opportunity to make known the truths of the Gospel to a vast uncommitted audience outside the Church! He found the Bishops evasive, however; nor did a visit to a Roman Catholic priest or a famous theological library or a Sunday service of worship bring him any nearer to the object of his search. Through all the articles there runs the cynicism of a hard-boiled journalist combined with the wistful longing of a parent, and in the end he reaches the perfectly humanistic conclusion that only man's love is eternal and only man's love can make this world safe and happy for generations to come.

Norman Price can find very little of value in organized religion. It is obvious that he considers the Church lamentably behind the times, hopelessly irrelevant, dismally uninteresting and tragically insensitive to the real problems of man and society in the modern age. He does write appreciatively, however, of certain representatives of the Church. For example, he visited one clergyman, the rector of a parish on the south-east waterfront, an ex-naval officer and Olympic athlete who gave up a cushy position to tackle one of the roughest church jobs in London. This man's rugged honesty and sacrificial commitment impressed him. He describes him as "a front line soldier in his own invisible war, poorly paid and needing sleep". "What keeps such a man going?"

he asks. "Not the money. He would make more on the buses. So it must be faith." Norman Price admits that though next Sunday will not find him in church "among the bobbing bonnets, whining and cajoling to a Father Image to save him from the Bogeyman", yet he would like to have such faith as that which kindles the flame of purity and dedication in the eyes of the parish priest.

The one valid argument for Christianity is still a Christian character. The man outside the Church may be critical of Christian theology and Christian institutions; he may be willing to argue along the lines of a debate held in the London School of Economics, that "organized religion is the most pernicious influence in modern society"; but unless he is a confirmed cynic who projects his own base motives into everyone he meets, then the sight of one consecrated Christian will at least temper, if not silence his criticism. The one thing which he respects in a Christian, or in any man, is sincerity, a life that rings true.

Strangely enough, some of these worldly characters are the ones who get most upset when their Christian idols turn out to have feet of clay. They respect sincerity, but it sometimes shakes them and certainly hardens them in their opposition to organized religion when they meet professedly religious people whose lives do not ring true. In facing up to the obstacles which prevent many honest doubters from moving forward and wholeheartedly accepting the Christian Faith, we must certainly consider as such an obstacle the failure of Christians themselves to live up to what they profess. Many a man feels repelled rather than attracted by the Church because, as he declares, not unpiously, "There are too many hypocrites in the Church!"

No attempt should be made to answer this objection in people who themselves are not sincere and who say with a kind of smug satisfaction, "The Church is full of hypocrites!", no reply except, "You had better come in, brother; there is always room for one more!" Nor shall we convince those faint-hearted folk who purposely exclude themselves from the Church for fear of what their friends and neighbours might expect of them. We are simply trying to meet the very reasonable objection in the minds of many seekers-for-truth who might be encouraged to give the Christian Faith an honest trial in their lives, except that they look at those of us who call ourselves Christians, at what we profess and at what we are, and they see a wide gulf fixed between the two. It disturbs them that the moral fruits of Christianity sometimes flourish more abundantly outside the Church than in it; and when we invite them to join us, they feel justified in asking, "What do ye more than others?"

What shall we say to the man who finds the hypocrisy of Christian people a stumbling-block in his spiritual pilgrimage? First, we shall remind him that he will not escape the atmosphere of hypocrisy by excluding himself from the community of religious faith. Hypocrisy is a human failing by no means restricted to Christianity. You find hypocrites in a Jewish synagogue, in a Hindu temple or in a Moslem mosque. You find hypocrisy outside religion altogether, even among godless peoples who sometimes make it a weapon of diplomacy. Abraham Lincoln warned his fellow-countrymen that the logical outgrowth of slavery would be a society that discriminated against all human minorities, and he said, "When it comes to this, I shall prefer emigrating to some country where they make no pretence of loving liberty, where despotism can be taken pure, and without the base alloy of hypocrisy."

Three years ago a small city in eastern Canada announced its plans to hold a bullfight—not the sort they have in Spain where the bull is killed, but the sort they have in Portugal where the bull is only goaded and filled with darts by a man on horseback. Many people wrote angry letters to the newspapers deploring this cruelty as unworthy of "the finest traditions of sport which exist in Canada", letters which, according to one editorial writer, contained "a considerable element of unlovely smugness plus a pompous hypocrisy". Under our "finest traditions of sport," he said, "we permit young men to go into a prize ring and batter each other's brains out . . . We have 'brave hunters' and 'sportsmen' licensed by law to shoot down defenceless deer . . . We have that glory of sport called 'wrestling' where cruelty is applauded hysterically even when it is faked." The writer concluded, "There are things in life almost as unlovely as cruelty. Among them is boastfulness over a virtue that is non-existent—and the ugly sin of hypocrisy."[1]

You need not enter a church in order to meet hypocrites;

[1] The Ottawa *Journal*, June 26th, 1958.

they flourish in all areas of secular society. Any man is a hypocrite who professes one code of conduct and condones or actually engages in another. The man who takes solemn marriage vows and gives the appearance of a model husband and father, but carries on an affair with one of the girls at the office, that man, though he may never darken the door of a church, is still a hypocrite; and that is the kindliest thing we can say about him. The woman who exudes sweetness and charm in public and acts like an untamed she-wolf in her own home, though she may have no use for religion, is still a hypocrite. The international spy is a hypocrite, and so is the office spy who gives his right ear to the boss and his left ear to his colleagues and tries to play each off against the other. To find large-scale hypocrisy look in the professional world or the world of business, labour relations, politics, journalism, art or diplomacy. You will not necessarily excuse the Church because of it, but you will realize that people bring to religion the same human weaknesses that they bring to all their relationships, and because the Church is composed of weak human beings, it is therefore an institution shot through with hypocrisy.

We must say also that the hypocrisy of Christian people does not invalidate the Faith itself. The existence of poor Christians no more discredits Christianity than the existence of careless motorists discredits the internal combustion engine. An intelligent man will not wash his hands of English literature simply because a few authors have glorified immorality; or stop going to the theatre because an actress who has just divorced her fourth husband plays the role of a Christian saint; or declare science a work of the Devil because some scientists have conducted unworthy experiments. No sensible man judges any area of reality—business, industry, science, politics, culture, or religion—on the basis of its weakest representatives, or even in terms of what people have made of it at all. He looks at the reality itself, its history, its accomplishments, its place in human life, and its future possibilities, and on that broad basis he forms his appraisal.

This delightful story comes from the mission field in Angola. Candolo was a thief; the Africans would call him a "great Thief", because his thieving was a profession which had been handed down from father to son like a medieval craft. Late one night he found himself on the trail and decided to ask shelter at a nearby village until the morning. This was a Christian village, so the villagers received him courteously, and when they learned that he came from Camundongo, the headquarters of the mission station, they brightened visibly. "Ah, we are indeed honoured to have an elder from Camundongo visit our village." Candolo thought of the goat he had stolen a few days previously. "How fortunate darkness should put a good man from Camundongo amongst us!" Candolo thought of the bicycle he had stolen from a Portuguese trader and resold to an unsuspecting African teacher. "It is many moons since we had a visitor speak to us of the Gospel. Will you speak to us in the prayer house?" The stolen cloth on his back began to itch unpleasantly, and Candolo tried to explain that he was most unsatisfactory as a guest speaker. "But you are from Camundongo!" With sinking heart he realized that they identified him with the pastors, the catechists, the deacons, the teachers and the devoted laymen of Camundongo. What was he to do? What was he to say? "I'm sorry. I'm just an old thief." How would that sound? Suddenly he was filled with a fierce desire to protect the good name of Camundongo. They proceeded to the prayer house, and Candolo, being a bit of a Christian himself, gave those villagers that evening a resounding sermon on the Good Life. He gave it straight and to the hilt, and the elders delivered thanks that their small village had had the fortune to have such a speaker as its overnight guest. Some days later old Candolo turned up at the missionary house. His face was drawn, for his soul was carrying a heavy burden. He told the missionary all about his session at the village and how he had tried to protect the name of Camundongo. But he had got to thinking how *he*, a thief, had stood up and preached the Word of God! Surely this must be a most dreadful sin? The missionary, who must have struggled to hide a smile, told Candolo that the Word had suffered a great many trials and had proved very tough. He doubted that it would be greatly impaired by the one-night stand in a village. Who knows, it might even have gained something from a rugged heart![1]

That is the answer to the man who says that there are

[1] As told by Munroe Scott in *African Manhunt*. Published by the Board of Information and Stewardship of the United Church of Canada, Toronto 1959, pp. 64–66.

too many hypocrites in the Church. There have always been hypocrites in the Church in every generation since the earliest days of Christianity. Read the letters of Paul, especially First Corinthians, if you want to see the sparks fly as this great Apostle scolds the early Christians for their hypocritical conduct. "You should be ashamed of yourselves!" he thunders at them. "Have you no decency that you bring the Faith into disrepute by your disgusting behaviour at the Lord's Table? You have made Christianity the laughing-stock of the whole world! What is the matter with you? Do you despise the Church of God that you act in this abominable way?" But Paul did not then wash his hands of the Corinthian Church and write off the Christian experiment as a failure. He knew that the Gospel is like music for which instruments have not yet been invented that can play it adequately, and he knew that the Gospel itself is tough and durable and will survive whatever people in any generation make of it.

It takes a certain courage to be a hypocrite. However we may deride hypocrisy it still presupposes idealism, and the hypocrite, though he may be unattractive, is a man who has taken a stand on high moral ground. There are two characters in the parables of Jesus who have suffered unfavourably by their comparison with other characters. First, the elder brother in our Lord's story of the Prodigal Son—that priggish person who reacted so petulantly to all the fuss being made over his brother's return, who would not join the homecoming party and who blurted out to his father, "Lo, these many years do I serve thee; yet thou never gavest me a kid that I might make merry with my friends!" Astonishing that he had any friends! Second, the Pharisee in our Lord's story of the Pharisee and the Publican—that self-righteous religious professional who catalogued his virtues before God and gave thanks that he was not like other men, "extortioners, unjust, adulterers, or even as this publican". In each case our sympathies go instinctively to the underdog. We excuse the prodigal and the publican by saying, "For all their waywardness and wickedness, at least they were not hypocrites." Surely, however, there is something worse than hypocrisy, and that is an outright rejection of all moral scruples and a turning of one's back on the commandments and the love of God. The elder brother and the Pharisee do seem hypocritical, but only because, having adopted high principles, they stand judged by those high principles.

Less cultured people sometimes throw up a defence-mechanism in the form of an inverted snobbery. Realizing that they cannot emulate the refinement of their social and intellectual superiors, they pretend to despise it instead and they glorify their own vulgarity in speech and manners. It is also possible to develop an inverted hypocrisy, a pretended contempt for that very moral refinement which we have neither the courage nor the will to imitate. You see this amply displayed in films and novels which deliberately distort the face of goodness and leave us feeling that the rogue or the scoundrel is really a very lovable person who deserves our understanding and our sympathy. We attach a virtue to not making a pretence of virtue. Alice Meynell has expressed that truth in her poem, "The Newer Vainglory".

> "Two men went up to pray; and one gave thanks,
>   Not with himself—aloud,
> With proclamation—calling on the ranks
>   Of an attentive crowd.
>
> 'Thank God, I clap not my own humble breast,
>   But other ruffians' backs,
> Imputing crime—such is my tolerant haste—
>   To any man that lacks.
>
> 'For I am tolerant, generous, keep no rules,
>   And the age honours me.
> Thank God, I am not as these rigid fools,
>   Even as this Pharisee.' "[1]

There is no doubt that some people do actually regard the hypocrisy of Christians as a barrier to their full acceptance of Christianity. But why? Let them inquire into the root of their apprehension, and they will find it to be less a criticism of Christians than a vindication of Christianity itself. In one sense we compliment a Christian when we call him a hypocrite, because we thereby acknowledge that, as a Christian, he should identify himself with a higher level of moral excellence than society commonly expects of its members. Instead of being content to succeed on the level of

---

[1] Quoted in *Masterpieces of Religious Verse*, Ed. James Dalton Morrison, Harper and Brothers Publishers, New York and London, 1948, p. 397.

conventional respectability, such a man has the courage to fail and to be accused of hypocrisy for his failure in attaining to the exalted level of Christ. He has the spirit of Browning's "Grammarian",

> "That low man seeks a little thing to do,
> Sees it and does it:
> This high man, with a great thing to pursue,
> Dies ere he knows it."

The Church is full of hypocrites, but the Church is the first to recognize it. There was a minister who ascended his pulpit one Sunday and greeted the congregation by saying, "Good morning, sinners!" Perhaps he should have said, "Good morning, fellow-sinners!" He then proceeded with an inspiring discourse on the strange fact that the Christian Church is the only organization in the world whose members meet together regularly to advertise themselves as "miserable sinners". The Church is the one organization with no place in its membership for perfect people. In the fourth century in North Africa there was a Christian sect known as Donatists who dedicated themselves to preserving the moral purity of the Church in the midst of an immoral environment and who became so engrossed with manicuring their own souls that they developed a spiritual snobbery and firmly believed themselves to be a society of perfect people. The Church repudiated Donatism, however, as it has always repudiated that heresy in the name of him who "came to seek and to save that which was lost". The Church is not and never has been a society of saints; and to condemn Christianity because some of its adherents confess that "there is no health in them" would be like condemning a hospital because many of its patients are confined to bed. The Church is indeed a hospital for spiritually sick people, and we have our Physician.

Two girls stood in a great art gallery before a famous painting. One whispered to the other, "I am not so impressed. What do you think of it?" Overhearing her, the guide said, "Lady, that masterpiece is not on trial before you; you are on trial before that masterpiece." The same reply could be made to the man who stands outside the Church looking critically at this imperfect but eternal fellowship which reaches back through the centuries to the

138

early apostles, to Christ himself, and to the very heart of God. "The Church is not on trial before you. The Church and the world outside the Church are on trial before God, because far more heinous than the hypocrisy of one professing Christian is the sin of all mankind that stands judged before the Cross." The Christian does not argue with the man who accuses him of hypocrisy, because the Christian lives a life that is precisely under the sign of the Cross. He takes that man's sin and his own sin and brings it to the place where sin is revealed in its depth and enormity and where alone it can be forgiven.

Someone has said, "It may be that a lot of superstition, it may be that a lot of conservative prejudice, clings to the historic Churches; but superstition and prejudice are the grime upon the pavement of what is still a *sacred* building; and he who would wash that pavement clean must be willing to get down on his knees to his work *inside* the Church." Even imperfect pillars within the Church can do more to hold up the Church than those who merely support it like buttresses from outside. Beyond a certain spurious feeling of moral superiority, what does a man gain and what does he contribute by dissociating himself from the company of hypocrites? To be sure, he may live a life of high integrity and unselfish service, but, as J. H. Oldham writes, "must he not ask himself whether, by withholding his allegiance, he may not be weakening the influence of the one historic institution formed on the belief that love has been manifested as the ultimate meaning of the universe?"

An audience of ministers and laymen listened to a stirring address by a missionary from Angola, whose father had been a missionary in Angola, and who passionately pleaded for support of the Church in its crucial role in Africa today. In the discussion period that followed, an angry young man, the sort who had scarcely begun to shave, rose to his feet and expressed dissatisfaction with the stodginess and hypocrisy of the Church. He said that there were too many hypocrites in Church pews, people who appropriated the benefits of Christianity without paying the price of Christianity. This conference was typical—Talk! Talk! Talk! But what were we going to do about it all? Quietly the missionary replied, "Well, I shall tell you what I am going to do. I am going back to Africa. What are you going to do?"

Christ would have looked on this young man and loved him, loved him for his vitality and his warm, mercurial discontent. It breaks the great heart of Christ that his army is indeed filled with soft parasitical soldiers who are unworthy to be called by his name; but it also breaks his heart that so many magnificent people stand hesitatingly on the sidelines and will not enlist in his war against evil. This incident from the war answers the man who finds the hypocrisy of Christian people a stumbling-block to his faith. After V-Day a platoon of Allied soldiers in Europe came to a bombed-out church. At the high altar they saw that the figure of Christ had been smashed, but by searching around, they gathered the pieces and cemented them together — all but the hands. These could not be found anywhere. So one soldier wrote something on a placard and left it by the partly-restored statue of Christ. It read, "He has no hands but yours."

13

The Failure of Christianity

IN 1939 a world organization known as the League of
Nations went out of business. It had been a noble experiment in peace-making; its fine headquarters in Geneva
symbolized the hope of a world capable of resolving its
disputes without the resort to armed force. The League of
Nations represented a colossal investment in money and in
dedicated human lives, and no one will question that for a
time it served a useful purpose and enjoyed a limited success.
Basically, however, it failed, because in 1939 the flames of
world conflict, which had been hitherto kept in check, broke
loose again with uncontrolled destructive fury. So the conference on fire prevention came to an end; men were too
busy fighting fires; and though for a time the League retained
its headquarters and kept up the appearance of an organization, yet essentially it had had its chance and failed, and the
world wrote it off as a failure.

Many people are convinced that the Christian religion,
as embodied in the organized churches, will reach, indeed
may be reaching even now, the same pathetic conclusion.
They believe that Christianity, as a way of life for mankind
and as an answer to the world's problems, has failed. And
they consider this to be an unbiased judgment. After all,
the League of Nations had only two decades in which to
civilize the human race. Christianity has had two millenniums, nineteen hundred years of unlimited freedom and
opportunity during which time it has enjoyed every support
that man can give it, the support of law, culture, wealth and
public opinion. What other religion or ideology has ever
possessed centres of propagation strategically placed at every
crossroads in more than half the world, and what other
religion or ideology has borne less fruit in proportion to its
numerical size and opportunity? To be sure, Christianity has
enriched countless lives and communities and may claim
limited victories through the centuries, but looking at the

decidedly unchristian character of the world today, we can only conclude that as a universal way of life and as a means of solving our really important problems Christianity has had its chance and failed.

Thus we encounter another obstacle to Christian belief, another barrier which deters many people from considering seriously the claims of the Gospel. They feel that they are being asked to support a dying cause. There are cynics, of course, who prophesy the demise of Christianity with satisfaction, like the British free-thinker Bertrand Russell who has always viewed religion of any kind as "a disease born of fear and a source of untold misery to the human race". He believes that apart from fixing the calendar and enabling us to predict eclipses, religion has served no useful purpose and that its universal rejection would be the best thing that ever happened to the world, a sign that man is beginning to grow up. We shall not attempt to answer the cynics, because we doubt if their arguments will stand against the bar of reason, but we shall attempt to answer as convincingly as possible the honest seeker-after-truth who feels attracted to Christianity and yet bewildered and repelled by what appears to him as its failure.

Few passages from the Bible have greater relevance to our generation than the third chapter of the Second Epistle of Peter, especially his timely warning: "In the last days there will come men who scoff at religion and live self-indulgent lives, and they will say, 'Where now is the promise of his coming? Our fathers have been laid to their rest, but still everything continues exactly as it has always been since the world began.' "[1] Surely that describes our problem—the tormenting voice of scoffers, finding its echo in our own hearts, and telling us that nineteen centuries of Christianity have really made no difference in the story of mankind; the world is basically as evil as it was before the coming of Christ, so what further proof do we need that Christianity is false and inoperative? Evidently our problem is not new; it arose in the early Church, and while the arguments of the cynics concerned specifically the failure of Christ to come a second time in his glory, yet they apply with equal validity to what we consider to be the failure of Christianity to fulfil the purpose of Christ in his first coming. In answering these

[1] *New English Bible.*

arguments the writer of *Second Peter* tells his readers that they have lost sight of certain facts.

I

They have lost sight of the fact that everything has *not* continued exactly as it has always been since the world began. Let them look back over history and they will find some very drastic changes in the human situation, occurrences, events and crises which did not conform to the iron-clad law of uniformity. He reminds them of the Flood that destroyed all the world's inhabitants except the righteous Noah and his family. In those days people thought that things would go on and on, with business as usual, but one day—Crash! The heavens opened, the rains descended, washing away one civilization and cleansing the earth for another. Wherever it fits into the geological picture, the Flood bisected history, and Peter points to it as proof that crises do occur which break the historical process and change radically the situation of man on this earth.

We in our generation should be able to grasp the concept of radical change. We know what it means to enter a new age; some of us have done it twice in our lifetime. We know that life on this earth will never be the same again now that we have split the atom and moved into outer space. The New Testament places that construction on the advent of Christ, and for that reason history has been redated with reference to him. When Jesus of Nazareth first came into Galilee preaching the Gospel of God, he said, "The time has come; the Kingdom of God is upon you; repent and believe in the Gospel." The writers of the New Testament, recalling this proclamation in the light of the events of Christ's life and death and resurrection, concluded that with his coming a new order of life had indeed dawned for mankind. Once again by an act of God history had been bisected; a crisis had occurred which broke the historical process and radically changed the situation of man on this earth.

To deny that Christianity *has* changed the human situation is simply to ignore the history of the past nineteen centuries. Admittedly that change has not always been beneficial, but that is inevitable, because the presence of good always gives rise to new and more deadly forms of evil;

the best can always be corrupted; it can bring out the worst in men, as it did in the men who crucified Jesus. But read the story in its wholeness, study the record impartially, and you will be constrained to admit that while the highest ideals of Christianity may not have been realized, yet as a creative, transforming force in the life of men and society, Christianity has been phenomenally productive.

Two thousand years after his birth the world cannot forget that there once lived a man whose name was Jesus. There is the Christian Church to remind us. There is a realm of art, architecture, literature and music. There is a succession of saintly lives down the centuries, a magnificent tradition of unselfish devotion and service. There is a civilization influenced to some degree by Christian beliefs and principles. There is our own conscience which, to a far greater extent than we realize, reflects the teaching and example of Jesus; and the conviction, now widely held, that the things which Christ stands for, these and these alone are the things that make for peace. Read this telling appraisal of Jesus from the pen of an unknown disciple: "I am far within the mark when I say that all the armies that ever marched, and all the navies that ever sailed, and all the parliaments that ever sat, and all the kings that ever reigned, put together, have not affected the life of man upon this earth as has that one solitary life."

So now we are told to repudiate the religion of Jesus, but what alternatives shall we offer in its place? "How can Christianity be true," people exclaim sadly, "when the hideous and diabolical world scene shows it up as so utterly impracticable? Obviously Christianity has not worked!" We reply, Then what has worked? This demonic regime of anti-Christianity, this worship of money and power and politics, this diplomacy filled with falsehood, this reliance on war to settle human differences, this fanatical faith in weapons of mass annihilation — have these worked? Surely the tragedy of the world does not rule out Christianity as a failure; rather it rules out these humanistic alternatives and vindicates Christianity as the one hope that still remains to the individual and society.

Peter reminds his readers that there is another fact of which we must not lose sight when we feel tempted to talk about the "failure" of Christianity — the fact that with God "one day is like a thousand years and a thousand years like one day". We tend to believe that the religion of Jesus is now hoary with age and that nineteen centuries should be ample time for it to change completely the character of life upon this earth. We forget that God's holy purposes do not follow a railway time-table or operate according to a factory time-clock. He who has watched over the earth through the millenniums of centuries since it evolved from the cosmic star dust views time differently than we do, so that what seems like an eternity to us may be but a moment in the Divine reckoning.

Numerous comparisons have been advanced to show that in the larger perspective of the earth's history Christianity, far from having run its course, has barely got started. Sir James Jeans refers to Cleopatra's Needle, the ancient stone pillar that stands on the Thames Embankment in London, and he suggests that if a penny were placed on top of this pillar and on top of the penny a postage stamp, the thickness of the stamp and the penny added to the height of the pillar would represent the space of time during which the earth has been in existence; the thickness of the penny and the stamp together represents the time during which man has been on the earth; the thickness of the stamp alone represents the time during which man has been civilized. To change the figure, if we reduce the five hundred million years during which life has been on this planet to the scale of one calendar year, we should find that from March to the middle of December the higher forms of living organisms appeared; man stood upright for the first time on the thirty-first of December at three o'clock in the afternoon; at eleven fifty-eight p.m., two minutes before midnight, Jesus came. Think of the same truth in terms of a man who in this year of our Lord celebrates his one hundredth birthday. It is a great age to attain, and he will receive a telegram from the Queen; but we need only set him alongside eighteen other centenarians who have gone before him, and those nineteen life-times, reaching back to Christ himself, represent the space of time during which we have expected Christianity to redeem this fallen earth and change it into a paradise.

Of course, we must reckon with the possibility that man's time may run out, because he now has it within his power, by wickedness or sheer folly, to bring his history to an abrupt end. We used to smile at Peter's bizarre description of the end of the age: "the heavens shall pass away with a great noise, and the elements shall melt with fervent heat"; but the great noise of which Peter had no inkling has actually been heard, and fervent heat has melted the bodies and the cities of men. Having projected himself some several thousand years forward in time and some several thousand light years away in space, an American newspaper editor wrote an imaginative article entitled, "Earth's Death, Seen from 45,000 A.D."; he concluded by saying that though evolutionary man had achieved much in both the material and spiritual realms, yet "in one incredible moment man renounced his goals, mocked at the flowering promise ahead of him, considered the ooze which he had worked a billion or two years to escape, and embraced it".

III

That dreadful possibility gives weight to another fact of which we lose sight when we become impatient with what seems like the failure of Christianity to solve the world's problems. Peter says, "It is not that the Lord is slow in fulfilling his promise, as some suppose, but that he is very patient with you, because it is not his will for any to be lost, but for all to come to repentance." If organized Christianity has been unfaithful to the redemptive commission of Christ, if the Church's record has been bad, no one is more conscious of it and more repentant than Christian leaders themselves. Let the critics read these trenchant words of Paul Tillich: "Religion, like all life, is ambiguous . . . It distorts what it has received and fails in what it tries to achieve. That is the tragedy of religion." Yet the New Testament does not allow us to lose faith in the ultimate triumph of Christ's Kingdom. It sees this delay, this period of apparent failure, as proof of the patience of God, as the opportunity which God has given the Church to preach the Gospel and bring all men into his

Kingdom. God does not wish that any of his children should perish; therefore he is stretching out the calendar, so to speak, that all might "come to repentance".

We shall not attempt to answer the precise question, Has Christianity failed? because we are really not competent to answer it. It is not we who judge the Gospel, but the Gospel that judges us. It was not Jesus on trial before Pontius Pilate, but Pilate on trial before Jesus; not Christianity on trial before Western civilization, but Western civilization on trial before Christianity. Does a man throw a new machine on the scrap heap and declare that it will not work because he lacks the intelligence to study the directions and follow them carefully and make the machine work? The Jews had a rabbinical saying that if they were penitent for one day, the Messiah would come. We can surely add that if for one day the Christian world really practised Christianity with some imagination and sacrifice, the Kingdom of God would come. Christianity has not failed us; we have failed Christianity; and the miracle of God's grace is that God still remains patient with us, still forgives our failures, still affords us every opportunity to bring men to repentance.

It is possible, of course, that God's patience, like man's time, may run out, and that God himself may be a jump ahead of his critics in closing the doors on this noble experiment of the centuries. The Bible makes it very clear that God always judges most severely those who call themselves his people, and that no religious institution, whatever its antiquity, will be allowed to survive when it fails to serve the Divine purpose. Jesus spoke that warning in many of his parables — the Barren Fig Tree that yielded nothing but leaves; the Great Feast where the invited guests refused to come and their places were taken by the rabble of the streets; the Wicked Husbandmen driven out of the vineyard and replaced by worthier tenants who would give the owner the fruits in their season. It does not lie within our competence to write off Christianity as a failure, but it certainly lies within God's competence; and God may do exactly that if the Church proves unworthy of its stewardship; he may reject all the visible institutions of Christianity and seek new vehicles, new forms of expression for his everlasting Gospel.

Meanwhile, however, the Church is living in the time of God's patience, a crisis that contains not only the element

147

of danger but also the element of opportunity. Relating his experiences an Air Force pilot told a friend how in the days of training he had been instructed in the use of a parachute but had never actually used one. Then the time came in combat over Germany when his plane was struck and it burst into flames. He said, "I knew that I had to bale out. I couldn't pull the string at once because I was surrounded by enemy planes, and I had to fall, waiting until I fell into the clouds before pulling the cord." His friend said in amazement, "I don't see how you could do it, never having done it before." "Well, that's simple," replied the pilot, "I had to do it. It was my only chance." We do well to pause before rejecting Christianity as having failed our civilization; we may be rejecting the only chance that God has given us to save our civilization from falling to a certain death.

IV

The writer of *Second Peter* calls to mind another fact of which we lose sight in our readiness to pass judgment on the apparent failure of Christianity. He says, "We have this promise, and look forward to new heavens and a new earth, the home of justice." Consider the basis of this obstacle to Christian belief. We have difficulty accepting the truth of the Christian Gospel because we are dissatisfied with the fruits of nineteen centuries of Christianity and because, looking at the non-christian character of our world, we feel that as a way of life and as an answer to the world's problems Christianity has not succeeded. How, then, shall we define success? Suppose all our expectations were fulfilled, what should we hope to see? Presumably a world at peace, where all the problems that bedevil modern life, the problems of hunger and misery and poverty and war and discrimination would be eliminated, a world where there would be equal opportunity for all and where men would live together harmoniously in freedom and security and dignity and prosperity—in short, an earthly utopia.

But surely Christianity has no monopoly on this goal of an earthly paradise. Visionaries and philosophers have dreamed of it and written about it with no reference to the motives and ideals of religion at all. Every political party makes better social conditions the principal plank of its election platform; and in this regard some marvellous advances have been made in social responsibility over the past few years. What could be more desirable than the peaceful goals which Mr. Khruschev holds before the Russian people, his twenty-year plan that will give every worker a thirty-two-hour week, a fair wage and an equal share in the world's wealth? But see what happens to men when they have no vision beyond this earthly utopia; they panic and resort to coercion and violence in order to achieve it. They declare war on generations of unborn children by polluting the earth's atmosphere with the deadly fall-out of fifty-megaton bombs and, dedicated to the establishment of heaven on earth, they end up by creating a hell instead.

Suppose that Christianity does in fact succeed, as we should like to see it succeed; suppose that somewhere in the remote future our hopes come to fruition and we bring forth upon this earth an order of life controlled entirely by the teachings of Jesus. Does that mean that the strivings of the centuries have been nothing but preparation for the final event, the inevitable casualties that go into the winning of a war? Does it mean that we shall have removed the last vestiges of evil from man's nature, so that it shall no longer be possible for him to cancel in half a generation, as he has often done in the past, the moral achievements of centuries? Scientists tell us that ultimately the planet earth, which had a beginning in time, will come to an end in time, even if we do not hasten that end prematurely. Some day this terrestrial ball will shrivel up and die. What happens then to the earthly paradise which the millenniums have agonized to bring forth? It all means that in judging the success or failure of Christianity we must be able to look beyond our limited human goals to goals which endure, beyond the things which are seen and temporal to things which are unseen and eternal.

The New Testament helps us to do that. "We have this promise," writes Peter, "and we look forward to new heavens and a new earth, the home of justice." The Church's Gospel has never looked forward to an ideal human situation within the bounds of history; it has never pretended that the earth can become a paradise. As Jesus told us, weeds will always infest the wheat field, evil growing alongside the good, more subtly and insidiously, perhaps, because, as we have seen, the presence of the best always brings out the worst. The New Testament, however, sees an end of this struggle between light and darkness, sees beyond history to a new situation, not created by man but given by God; not the old earth refurbished, but a new earth, a new Jerusalem "coming down from God out of heaven prepared as a bride adorned for her husband".

v

Hence the final fact which Peter recalls for his readers and for all of us who feel that the unhappy state of affairs in our world throws doubt on the claims of the Christian Gospel. "Do not lose your own safe foothold," he writes, "but grow in the grace and in the knowledge of our Lord and Saviour Jesus Christ." Peter is telling us that as Christians we are not called upon to run the universe. God has his own strategy, his own time-table; and we are called simply to remain faithful in our own lives and to be certain that we do not make what seem like obstacles to belief an excuse for disobedience. Christianity will succeed because it is God's revealed truth and because in raising Jesus Christ from the dead God has assured us of his ultimate victory over all the powers of death and hell. We hasten that victory, which shall be our victory, by applying ourselves faithfully to the tasks which God has appointed to us here and now. We can say with Albert Schweitzer, "However great the world's evil, I never allow myself to get lost in brooding over it. I always hold firmly to the belief that each of us can do a little to bring some portion of it to an end. Because I have faith in the power and truth of the Spirit, I believe in the future of mankind."

14

A Church Divided

IN HIS initial discussions with the Church leaders in 1950 Mr. Chou En-lai, the Premier of Communist China, said that denominational distinctions must go and the churches must unite. In 1958 the government ordered the Chinese churches to effect organic union. To enforce this regulation the government promptly closed many houses of worship. Peking, the capital, which had had eighty churches, was left with four, one for each point of the compass; thus releasing a great deal of church personnel and property for the state in its all-absorbing drive for industrial power. It is known that the Anglican Cathedral in Peking was turned into a factory. On the first Sunday following the enforced union sermons were preached from all pulpits in the new "re-formed" and "united" Church which called for rejoicing in the light and blessing that had now come to Christians in China.

Many people wish that the churches in our Western world could be taken by the scruff of the neck and forced to resolve their differences. They would like to see the government or some other external authority bring the bishops and moderators and chairmen and presidents together and present them with an ultimatum to unite or else . . . Meanwhile their own attitude remains one of intimidation. There are many things about Christianity that they do not like, but chiefly they look with disgust on the spectacle of a divided Church; and so long as the Church remains divided, they self-righteously refuse to have anything to do with it. The sight of Protestants and Catholics, Liberals and Evangelicals, Anglicans and Freechurchmen barking at one another like paranoids in a mental hospital appals them, so they take refuge in agnosticism and declare with the dying Mercutio, "A plague o' both your houses!"

Others are frankly puzzled. They want to believe the truth of the Christian Gospel, because they see in it hope for their own lives and for the world's problems, but the Gospel has so many conflicting interpretations that they do not know which to believe and accept. They might listen to the Faith as to a sweet theme of music, but they can hardly discern the theme when the churches march past like a parade of brass bands, each trying to drown out the others with its own variations. Religion, which should be the supremely reconciling force in life, appears to them as one of the great divisive influences in our society. They remember that the bloodiest wars have been wars of religion; they see less fraternity among priests than among politicians; and they see their friends, who can walk together into the same public house, compelled to walk separately into different houses of God. The disunity of Christians constitutes a barrier to their own belief; they feel that there must be something deficient about a faith which drives people apart and makes them intolerant of each other when concern for the common decencies would otherwise unite them. They ask, "How can a Church split into competing fragments, each claiming to be The True Church, each claiming to have a monopoly on the whole truth, each regarding the others with such bigotry and bitterness, possibly be reconciled with the spirit of love and sacrifice in the New Testament?"

The answer is that it cannot and should not be reconciled with the New Testament. The person who stands outside the Church and pokes ridicule at its divisions comes closer to the truth of the Gospel than the person who sits inside the Church and says that the divisions do not matter. Divisions do matter, and nobody emphasized that more plainly than did the Apostle Paul in his sometimes vitriolic letter to the *Corinthians*. Paul had founded a church in Corinth, a little fellowship of believers bound together, so he thought, by their common faith in one Lord and Saviour, Jesus Christ; but scarcely had the apostle turned his back than these people began resolving themselves into factions, each calling itself by the name of some man or party, each fixing on one facet of Christian truth and arrogantly claiming it to be the whole truth. To Paul this could only mean that the Corinthians had never grasped the essential truth of Christianity at all. They were just worldly men imposing their unredeemed human weaknesses on the revelation of God.

"Is Christ divided?" he flung in their faces. "Was Paul crucified for you?" . . . or for that matter, was Peter or Athanasius or Martin Luther or John Calvin or John Wesley or any other religious leader by whose name men still call themselves? When we can take the historic Christ and carve him up like a carcase of meat, then only shall we be allowed to commit the blasphemy of carving up his Body, the Church.

The historic Jesus *willed* the unity of his Church. On the night before his crucifixion, as he comforted the sorrowing disciples in the Upper Room, he lifted his face to heaven and offered one sublime prayer for them and for all their spiritual descendants—"that they may all be one; even as thou, Father, art in me, and I in thee . . ." For his Church Christ willed the perfect unity of the Godhead, and he willed it for a purpose—"so that the world may believe that thou hast sent me . . ." Jesus saw even then that division within his Church would be a stumbling-block to people's faith, a violent contradiction of the Church's nature and an impediment to its mission. Christ came to reconcile men to God; he entrusted that ministry of reconciliation to the Church; but he knew that Christians can never be ambassadors reconciling a lost world to God if they themselves have not been willing to be reconciled to one another. Therefore he prayed and still prays that his Church may be one; and that we should settle for anything less than perfect unity is more than a scandal, it is a sin.

It might be helpful to consider how the Church came to be divided in the first place, even as early as the year A.D. 65. We have seen from the situation in Corinth that it was very largely an outgrowth of human nature. Humanity differs in all other respects—racially, politically, ideologically, temperamentally and culturally; logical, therefore, that religion, which is of all human characteristics the most universal, should be subject to human differences. All men do not agree on the same thing, or all men would be in love with the same woman; and since the truth of God's revelation in Christ is bound up with man's interpretation of it, that truth will naturally be presented to the world in different ways. A variety of interpretations do not invalidate the truth itself, however; they only show how instinctive and irrepressible the search for the truth is. Let it be admitted that those who desire an excuse for rejecting religion can find it in the division of Christendom, just as those who want a pretext for giving up food or medicine can find it in the diversities of dietetic or medical theories. We need food, however, and we need medicine regardless of how widely doctors disagree. We need religion as well, the healing, restoring medicine of Jesus Christ, regardless of how and by whom it is dispensed.

When we consider the historical situation that changed the word "Church" into a multiplicity of churches, we find the causes to be reasonable enough. Outwardly the Church was united for the first ten centuries, but in 1054, mainly for political reasons, the Eastern Church with its headquarters at Constantinople and the Western Church with its headquarters at Rome each decided to set up its own administration. After that, the Western Church fell on bad days and became so corrupt and worldly that devout and honest men began proposing reforms. The reformation took place in the sixteenth century, but it took place under different leaders, in different countries and at different times: in Germany under Luther, in Switzerland under Calvin and Zwingli, in England under Cranmer. Under the impulse of the Renaissance and the Industrial Revolution and with the opening of the New World, these forms of Christianity sub-divided and emigrated, the divisions often being caused less by theological than by racial, social and economic factors. In no case did any group set out to found a different religion than the religion of Jesus Christ in loyalty to the Word of God. Eastern Orthodox, Roman Catholic, Anglican, Lutheran, Presbyterian, Baptist, Methodist, Congregationalist, despite claims to the contrary, are not different trees growing in a forest, but branches of the same tree growing from the trunk of a single Gospel and rooted in the soil of God's revelation in Christ.

We have not exhausted the truth by saying cynically that the Church is divided. There is a sense in which the Church remains eternally united, and neither Christians themselves nor the critics outside the Church should be allowed to forget it. Even Paul, impatient as he was with arrant sectarianism, could still in his Letter to the Ephesians insist on the Church's essential unity, its oneness in Christ. "There is one body and one Spirit, just as you were called to the one hope that belongs to your call, one Lord, one faith, one baptism, one God and Father of us all . . ." Paul is saying that the churches, however they vary in order and tradition, are still a part of the one structure, founded on the one constitutive event; they still have a common origin in a Stable in Bethlehem, a Cross on Calvary, an Empty Tomb in Joseph's Garden. Paul is saying that, however divergent their interpretations, the churches still draw their sustenance from a common source of life—the Lord who gives his body to be broken and his blood to be shed in the sacrament of his Holy Table. Paul is saying that, however diverse their testimonies, the churches are engaged in the one apostolic mission, and whether there be too many churches or not, they still have a common purpose—to continue the reconciling ministry of Christ. Paul is saying that however high the fences around the Lord's Table, it is still *His* table, still the symbol of a common hope that beats in the hearts of all who love him—the hope of his eternal banquet in the Kingdom of God.

Nowhere does the essential unity of the Church become more visible than in the pages of a hymn book. How utterly impoverished our common worship would be if each congregation confined itself to hymns composed only by members of its own communion. Instead the hymns reach across the ages. They come from the Fathers of the East or the West in the early centuries; they come from the Middle Ages and from the Reformation; they come from stalwart High Anglicans and from Puritan Nonconformists; they come from the Wesleyan Revival and from the Society of Friends. When we sing the praises of Jesus,

> "Jesus, the very thought of thee
> With sweetness fills my breast,"

it is the monk Bernard who leads our song. When we offer a prayer for guidance,

> "Lead Kindly Light, amid the encircling gloom,
> Lead Thou me on,"

it is the Roman Catholic Cardinal Newman who leads our song. When we sing of our duty to foreign lands,

> "From Greenland's icy mountains,
> From India's coral strand,"

it is the Anglican Bishop Heber who leads our song. When
we sing of the Cross,

> "In the Cross of Christ I glory,
> Towering o'er the wrecks of time,"

it is actually the Unitarian, Sir John Bowering, who leads
our song. Isaac Watts was never allowed to preach in West-
minster Abbey, but scarcely an important function takes
place there except they sing Isaac Watts's great paraphrase:

> "O God, our help in ages past,
> Our hope for years to come."

That is the Church — not Roman, not Anglican, not Presbyterian, not Methodist, not Congregationalist, not Salvation
Army, but bigger and grander and nobler than all of these;
a glorious fellowship of loving souls who worship the one
Father God, who serve the one Lord and Saviour Christ,
who look for guidance and strength to the One Eternal
Spirit.

The essential unity of the Church makes itself known in
more dramatic ways. It is true that religion divides men
where common decencies tend to unite them; but this is far
outweighed by the fact that very often the one bond of fellowship that crosses all other barriers of race, nation and class,
the one link between men on both sides of the Iron Curtain is
their love and loyalty to a common Saviour. How true this
proved to be after the war when men who had been enemies
and who had destroyed each other's families and homes
faced the difficult task of reconciliation. In 1945 a deputation
from the Church in America went to re-establish contact
with the Church in Japan. The Americans harboured mis-
givings as to how they would be received, for regardless of
the issues out of which the war had emerged, they were
citizens of a conquering country whose armed forces had
wrought unprecedented havoc. What took place is best
expressed in these words describing the first Communion
Service which Americans and Japanese held together after
the war:

"Little can be said about the Communion itself. It was like any
other and yet unlike any other. The familiar words were read and
spoken, but through them all were overtones of repentance,
triumph and hope which gave us knowledge that the Gospel had

overcome national difficulties and enmities and that nothing, simply nothing, could in the end prevail against the Church of Christ."

Of course, that does not minimize, nor should it be allowed to minimize the fact that the Church, this fellowship of believers in Christ with such potential for bringing friend and foe together, stands before the world in a lamentably fragmented condition. No one deplores the scandal of the Church's disunity more than do Christian leaders themselves. As the late Bishop Berggrav said with masterly understatement, "Christendom as a whole today is having a bad conscience about unity in Christ." We in the Church know how hypocritical we must appear when we sponsor an ecumenical assembly of young people who study together, pray together and work together, but are not allowed to take Communion together at the Lord's Table. We know that the rivalry between Christians themselves has become far less important than the rivalry between Christians and non-Christians, and that just as a divided Church once fell before the sword of Islam, so a divided Church will be crushed under the steam-roller of Communism. We know that to boast of being united on the great issues but divided only on secondary matters makes fools of us, because it means that we are allowing secondary matters rather than the essentials to determine our life and policy. We know that division within the Church is more than human weakness, more than historical accident; it is sinful, a mutilation of the Body of Christ; it denies our faith, distorts our witness and frustrates our mission.

Quite understandably the man of the world will retort, "That's what I've been telling you all along. So why don't you get busy and do something about it? What is holding you back? Unite, and be done with it!" To the practical-minded layman it seems as simple as that, but unity is never that simple, even in the secular world. A group of business firms, because they manufacture the same product, because they already co-operate on certain levels, because they face stiff competition from producers of inferior goods, because they agree on basic methods of production, are not necessarily ready for a merger. Before they give up their separate identities, before organic union can be achieved, their basic disagreements must be frankly faced and resolved, else the merger is doomed to failure by its sheer superficiality. The churches are in an even more difficult position. Despite all their similarities, there are certain disagreements which have grown through the centuries and which strike to the depths of both thought and action; these hold the churches apart and will continue to do so until frankly faced and resolved. There can be no unity that simply means togetherness, because that will not last; nor can there be a unity that simply means absorption, because that were setting the stage to fight the same battles all over again. Paul gave the blueprint for unity in his Letter to the Ephesians when he expressed the hope that God would create "one new man in place of the two"—not an all-Protestant or all-Catholic Church, not an all-Anglican or all-Free Church, but a new being, a greater and more magnificent Church than we have ever dreamed. This will not come overnight, nor will it come easily, but only as the result of patience, prayer, labour and sacrifice.

That patience, that prayer, that labour and that sacrifice are taking place, despite the fact that many of the Church's critics are unaware of it. In 1958 Bertrand Russell allowed a collection of his essays to be published under the provocative title, *Why I Am Not a Christian*. The British philosopher has nothing but destructive criticism for religion in general and for Christianity in particular; and the Church he considers to be a reactionary and pernicious influence in society. The notable thing is that some of these essays were written half a century ago, and now they have been published without revision, indicating that in this respect, at least, the mind of this great man has not undergone a change in fifty years. How very typical of the Church's critics. Invariably they hold an outdated image, invariably they address themselves to a situation which may have ceased to exist. Those who deplore the division of Christendom seem quite unaware that the cardinal fact of the Church's life in the past half-century has been the concerted movement to end that division. The late Archbishop William Temple called it "the great new fact of our time".

Actually we are passing through one of the most thrilling eras in the history of the Church, an era which sees the dramatic reversal of that process of uncontrollable cell-division and multiplication which began four centuries ago to rend the fabric of the Church's life. Today churches, which from their inception have regarded one another with hostility or indifference, have begun seeking one another out, and in so doing have formed a new kind of Christian unity, more inclusive than that of the early Church, more vital than that of the Medieval Church. This "ecumenical" movement, or world-wide coming together of the churches, dates back to 1910 when officially accredited representatives of nearly all the major church families met at Edinburgh for a conference on the World Mission of the Church. This gave rise to the formation of the International Missionary Council which has not only consolidated work on the mission fields, not only fostered co-operation among the Western churches, but encouraged the creation of indigenous churches in mission lands themselves, and it is they who have furnished much of the impetus and leadership for the modern ecumenical movement.

This great new fact of our time has also found expression in the Faith and Order Movement. At Edinburgh in 1910 Bishop Charles Brent of New York made the suggestion that if the emerging unity were to be more than superficial, it must get down to the deeper level of theological agreements and differences. Several years elapsed before Bishop Brent's vision found fulfilment, but he did live to attend the first great Faith and Order Conference at Lausanne, Switzerland in 1927. Out of this and succeeding conferences grew the awareness that, despite all their differences, Reformation Christians are bound together by at least four basic convictions: belief in God who created the world and who governs the world in love; belief in Christ as the unique revelation of God to men, as the Saviour of the race and the living Lord of life and history; belief in man as a child of God, free to rebel against God, therefore sinful, but capable of new life through faith in Jesus Christ; belief in the Church as the Body of Christ, the Household of God, belief in the Church's Scripture, its ministry, its sacraments, and its historic mission as God's agent of redemption. The recognition of these basic theological agreements constitutes the very foundation of the Ecumenical Movement.

The great new fact has found expression in some exciting organic unions. Churches have been prepared to die, to lose their historic identity in obedience to the purpose of

159

God in order that God might raise them again to new and larger life. In 1925, after more than a quarter-century of conversations, Methodists, Presbyterians and Congregationalists in Canada merged to form the United Church of Canada—a new Church, a great ecumenical Church with its own body of doctrine, its own form of government, its own liturgies, its own ministry and its own mission at home and abroad. It is true to say that, like three strands of rope woven together in a stronger rope, the United Church of Canada has been able to undertake for God what the three denominations could never have undertaken separately. From a practical viewpoint, it has eliminated much needless overlapping, especially in the rural districts, and has made possible a more effective deployment of money and manpower, so that the Church's ministry might reach the more remote areas. Moreover, one senses in the new generation in Canada a pride in its threefold heritage, a sense of gratitude to God in belonging to a Church that combines the best of three traditions. Neither Paul, nor Apollos, nor Cephas, but "all things are yours".

The great new fact has found its highest expression in the World Council of Churches which came into being at Amsterdam on the 23rd day of August, 1948. On that day, for the first time in Christian history, there was instituted an official, permanent, world-wide fellowship of the churches dedicated to co-operation and unity. The World Council is not a super-Church, not a Protestant Vatican. It does not aspire to unite all non-Roman Catholics into one big denomination. The World Council is fundamentally a means by which the divided churches, partial in vision and limited in influence, may come together in fellowship in order to understand and appreciate one another, in order to pray and worship together, in order to study and discuss their common Christian responsibility toward the vital issues facing mankind. The work of its Department of Inter-Church Aid and Service to Refugees alone has been phenomenal. In 1953, one twelve-month period, it distributed some twenty-six thousand tons of food, clothing and medical supplies; established new homes for more than nineteen thousand refugee men, women and children; sent half a million pounds in cash for emergency help to victims of floods, earthquakes, fires and famine; and provided more than two million pounds for inter-Church and inter-Mission Aid projects throughout the world; and all this without political or ecclesiastical strings attached. In November of 1961 the World Council of Churches convened for its Third General Assembly in New Delhi, India where all divisions of race, nation and class, as well as those of Faith, Order and Tradition, were overcome as delegates from one hundred and seventy-seven Communions in sixty different countries reaffirmed their faith in *Christ, the Light of the World*, the only light that God has given to relieve the gross darkness that covers the earth.

Here, then, is the answer to that person who finds the scandal of a divided Church an obstacle to Christian belief. Division *is* a scandal, but it springs from understandable historic causes, and even though it does not compromise the essential unity of the Church in Christ, yet the churches are doing something about it in order that Christ's prayer, "that all may be one", shall be fulfilled and the Church on earth express the perfect unity of the Godhead. The only question for us to decide is whether we shall watch this thrilling drama of the Holy Spirit as spectators from the audience, or whether we shall step on the stage and play our parts.

15

The Challenge of Other Faiths

FROM the point of view of world Christianity, one of the most significant events in the past year has been the election of U Thant as Secretary-General of the United Nations Organization. U Thant is a practising Buddhist, a devout man who keeps a Buddhist shrine prominently displayed in his home. There is no reason, of course, why a Buddhist should not be appointed the world's number one civil servant; he was elected for his statesmanship, not for his religion. At the same time, we cannot help but contrast the present reaction of the Christian nations to this appointment with what would certainly have been the reaction a few generations ago. Our grandfathers, and more especially our grandmothers, would have been indignant over it. You can almost hear them, "A Buddhist? That means that he's not a Christian! He's one of the heathen!"

The fact, however, that this election could take place with universal approval is just another evidence of the new appreciation with which Christians regard other religious faiths. Pious people a century ago divided the human race into two groups, the Christians and the heathen, and they considered it the business of Christians to convert the heathen. Today every intelligent person knows that there are other religions besides Christianity, some of them older, with their own literature and culture, and that they have produced great characters and noble lives. Many factors have been responsible for this changed attitude—the study of comparative religions, the closer physical relationship between East and West, and the presence of Africans and Asians in our own country. We meet these people in our offices, our universities, our science laboratories, our places of business, we get to know them and admire them, and we are not quite so sure that we have a great deal of spiritual value to give them. Indeed we wonder if they might not have something to offer us.

That raises a question. Most of us were brought up to believe that, while there might be other religious faiths in the world, yet our faith was the only true one and that all others were definitely inferior. Now in these days which have seen a revival of interest in other faiths we find ourselves asking, Is Christianity the best religion, or is it simply one among equals, one facet of the larger truth, one finger on the hand of God? A man will say, "I feel no need of religion at all, but if I am going to be religious, why stop with Christianity? Why not study all the world's great ethnic faiths and take what is best from all of them?" Indeed what deters many people from looking more sympathetically at Christianity is precisely the arrogance with which Christianity does claim to be superior to other faiths. "I might embrace Christianity," adds the same man, "if it were not so intolerant, but I count among my friends a number of non-Christians, Jews, Muslims, agnostics, and I don't want to embarrass them. They have a right to their beliefs. Some of them are a lot finer than people who go to church. So until the Church wakes up and stops trying to convert them, I intend to remain outside the Church!"

An attempt to surmount the obstacles that prevent many good people from looking more sympathetically at the claims of the Christian Gospel must certainly include a consideration of the challenge of other religious faiths. After all, if the objections which we have just stated are valid, then it compels some serious rethinking of our Christian position, an honest re-assessment of our faith in its relation to other faiths. To do this effectively we should not only require a knowledge of the literature and philosophy of other religious systems, but we should need to get inside those systems and see what they mean to the people who believe in them; and we should certainly require a more thorough knowledge of our own religion. Such knowledge not many of us possess; if we did, we might have less to say one way or the other. Meanwhile, we try to confront this problem on the basis of what we do know, candidly and open-mindedly asking ourselves the question: What happens to the claims of Christianity in the light of our new appreciation of other religious faiths? Turning to the Bible for a positive answer, we derive some help from three passages in the New Testament.

First, the story of the Transfiguration. Shortly before Jesus set his face steadfastly to go to Jerusalem, knowing that there he would be crucified, he took three of his disciples up the side of a lonely mountain to join him in a season of prayer. There in a solitary place they had such an unusual experience that we should not believe it unless it were faithfully recorded as a first-hand account in three of the Gospels. As Jesus prayed, a light more dazzling than the sun enveloped him, so that his face and clothes shone with an unearthly brilliance. Staring at him, transfixed, the disciples suddenly saw two figures talking with him whom they instinctively knew to be Moses and Elijah. They must have been delirious with excitement. This could only mean that Jesus, whom they now believed to be God's Christ, had come into his glory, that God had exalted him and made him equal to the great representatives of Law and Prophecy; and Peter, ever impulsive and wanting to make this glory permanent, blurted out, "Lord, it is well that we are here; if you wish, I will make three booths here, one for you and one for Moses and one for Elijah."

You see what Peter would have done. He would have settled for a limited glory and been satisfied to claim for his Christ no more than equality with the great religious leaders of the past. Many moderns make the same limited response to the Gospel. That Christ should be one among equals, that he should take his place alongside Buddha, Mahomet, Confucius, Socrates—they are prepared to settle for that; but what they cannot accept is that Christ should claim to be more than other great religious leaders and that Christianity should style itself a unique religion, superior in its revealed truth.

This point of view finds support from some of the most outstanding thinkers of our day. Norman Cousins, the American journalist, believes that "there is a real need and opportunity for a World Parliament of Religions that will address itself to the human situation". He says, "Let the great religions cease explaining their differences to one another and begin to chart the elements of basic unity that would serve as building blocks of common action." Reinhold

Niebuhr has voiced doubts about the wisdom of missions to the Jews, declaring that in our attempt to proselytize God's Ancient People Israel we are depriving them of the distinctive contribution which they have to make to Western civilization. When Paul Tillich, the renowned theologian, lectured at Yale University in 1950 he dealt so profoundly and earnestly with other beliefs that the students published in their newspaper an article under the heading, "Will Tillich come out for Christianity?" Perhaps the most authoritative and articulate advocate of religious coexistence has been Arnold Toynbee, especially in the latest volume of his massive *Study of History* where he says, "I reject the pretension to be 'a Chosen People' in whatever people's name it is made . . . I reject the pretension of Christianity to be a unique revelation of the truth about Reality and a unique means of grace and salvation."

Toynbee is convinced that Christianity should be more tolerant of other faiths, and he objects strongly to the exclusive-mindedness that accompanies a belief in the uniqueness of our religion. We must certainly agree with him to a point; the assumption of an infallible religion or an infallible Church can lead to insufferable arrogance and egotism. What does Toynbee ask, however, when he pleads for tolerance? Does he mean that we should ignore the differences between our faith and others and that we should accept all religions as equally true and valid? The Hindus claim to be tolerant in this way: they will put statues of Christ in their temples and encourage the reading of some of the Christian Scriptures; they absorb what they consider to be the best of Christianity into their own system—which is surely not tolerance at all, but a kind of religious imperialism, fitting other people's faith into the straitjacket of your own. Surely tolerance in the highest sense means neither indifference nor absorption, but charity. The tolerant man will respect and try to understand people who differ from him, but he will not pretend that the differences do not exist, else he will not deserve *their* respect. The most tolerant Christians, with nothing but love in their hearts for men of every race and creed, have nevertheless known what they believed and have been so committed to their faith that they were willing to suffer and die for it.

What, in fact, do Christians believe? Let us come back

to the Transfiguration scene. To Peter's impulsive suggestion that Christ be given permanent equality with Moses and Elijah the voice of God spoke, "This is my beloved Son with whom I am well pleased . . . my beloved Son, not another prophet or lawgiver, not another religious leader in the long line of religious leaders, but my beloved Son, different in kind from all who have gone before him, the express image of myself in human form . . . listen to *him* !" Nineteen centuries ago a Man lived, was crucified and rose from the dead in far-away Palestine, and the constitutive truth of the New Testament is that God was in that life and death and resurrection. In that event which we call the "Christ-event" God, who created and governs this world, was supernaturally and conclusively acting for the world's salvation, and what God accomplished in Christ he accomplished for the whole world and for all men, including, as Augustine said, two-headed men and dog-headed men, if there were such creatures. Christianity does not present itself as the *only* truth about God and, in so doing, set out to destroy other religious faiths; if it did, it would be untrue to the New Testament. The New Testament believes that God has never left himself without a witness; through many inspired men he has spoken to the human race; but by speaking through his own Son God ratifies what others have said and he completes and brings to fulfilment all that has gone before.

Henry Van Dusen tells of a remarkable institution on the outskirts of Hong Kong, the most notable meeting-place of two great religions in the world.[1] Bearing in English the name, "The Buddhist-Christian Institute", it is a retreat or study centre where Buddhists, especially Buddhist priests, who wish to know more about Christianity, may come to live, to study, to reflect. They may return to their Buddhist vocations, or they may be baptized and even prepare for the Christian ministry. The buildings are all in the graceful style of a Chinese Buddhist monastery. At the heart stands the chapel, an octagonal structure focusing upon a simple altar in its centre. Above the altar there is the emblem of this fellowship, an open lotus-lily, the Buddhist symbol of unfolding truth; and above the lily hangs a Cross, signifying that Christianity does not destroy other faiths, but completes

[1] Henry P. Van Dusen, *Spirit, Son and Father* (Charles Scribner's Sons, New York, 1958), pp. 23–25.

them, and that in the Cross of Christ the living and present Spirit of Truth in all other religions may find fulfilment.

II

A second passage in the New Testament which enables us to face the challenge of other religious faiths occurs in the third and fourth chapters of *The Acts of the Apostles*. At the gate of the Temple in Jerusalem there sat a middle-aged beggar who had been lame from his birth and whose livelihood depended on the charity of people passing by. On this particular day the crowds were thronging past him when suddenly he noticed two men who must have appeared unusually sympathetic, and he reached out his hand for an alms. They stopped and looked at him, and their eyes were filled with compassion. One of them, named Peter, spoke, "I have no silver and gold, but I give you what I have; in the name of Jesus Christ of Nazareth, walk!" Peter took the outstretched hand of the beggar, lifted him to his feet, steadied him for a moment; and the poor creature, ecstatic with joy, leaped into the temple praising God.

For performing that little deed of mercy Peter and John were promptly clapped into prison by the religious authorities; not that they objected to the cure itself—they had some human feeling—but they did not like the sermon that Peter preached along with it. Next morning when the authorities interrogated their prisoners, they resorted to a very old and cheap trick, that of discrediting the deed by throwing suspicion on the source of its origin. They asked the disciples, "By what power or by what name do you do this?" "As if you didn't know," replied Peter in effect. "By the name of Jesus Christ of Nazareth, whom you crucified, whom God raised from the dead"; and to the dismay of the religious leaders Peter, the same Peter who once would have accepted for Christ a lesser glory than resurrection to God's right hand, preached another sermon which he concluded by saying, "And there is salvation in no one else, for there is no other name under heaven given among men by which we must be saved."

For nineteen centuries that has been the motive-power of Christianity—"no other name under heaven given among men by which we must be saved". Remove that conviction

167

and you remove the one impulse that kept Christianity alive through the persecution of the first three centuries, that inspired the writing of Gospels and Epistles, founded a Church, sent Paul on his journeys, took martyrs into the Roman Colosseum, and fired the missionary movement of the past two hundred years. Christians have felt divinely obligated to share with all men the truth of the Gospel, not because they wanted to bring the rest of the world around to their way of thinking, nor even because Christ himself commissioned them to "go into all the world and preach the Gospel to every creature", but because they believed that there is power at the heart of the Gospel, power in the name of Christ, power that can heal men, as it healed the wasted limbs of this Palestinian beggar, and raise them from paralysis to freedom and fulness of life.

What bothers Toynbee and other critics about the so-called "imperialism" of Christianity is that they see it as an attempt not only to Christianize but to Westernize Eastern people, thereby violating their cultural integrity. They seem to forget, however, that there are many things about Western culture which intelligent non-westerners are only too eager to have; our ways of defeating poverty, ignorance and disease, our schools, our hospitals, our systems of social service, our scientific and technical know-how. Many of these finer elements in our culture had their roots in the Christian Gospel, but is that a reason why we should not attempt to share them where they are needed and to share also the soil from which they have sprung? We believe that the Christian West has achieved a higher standard of life for its people *because* it has been Christian, because it has been motivated by a self-determination and social responsibility which are of the essence of Christianity; and if we are going to plead for a spirit of charity toward our brethren of other faiths, then it would be a queer expression of that spirit to withhold from them what God has given us, and the truth that God has given it to us, for fear of violating their cultural integrity.

In a little book bearing the title, *Is Christianity Unique?*[1] we read the following statement: "The tenets and practices of a living religion may be judged pre-eminently by the quality of life which they create in men." What quality of life does

[1] Nicol MacNicol.

Christianity create in men? Once the great Charles Darwin went to South America where he found a race of men who were little better than animals. Their minds were those of undeveloped children, their bodies were diseased and their surroundings were filthy. According to Darwin's theories, thousands and thousands of years must elapse before they could rise to the ordinary level of civilization. Years later Darwin went again to South America to visit these people who had interested him, and he could scarcely believe what he saw. They wore clothing now, they could read and write, they had schools and churches, and they were taking their place among other civilized peoples. The reason for this miraculous change? Missionaries had been there—the story of the lame man at the gate of the Temple all over again, a story which has been re-enacted through the centuries and around the world. That is Christianity's answer to the challenge of other faiths—not a claim to superiority, but simply that wherever the name of Christ has been preached society has been changed for the better, superstition has given way to enlightenment, and men have been raised from paralysis to freedom and fulness of life.

III

A third passage in the New Testament that enables us to meet the challenge of other religious faiths occurs in the second chapter of Paul's *Letter to the Philippians*. Paul knew about this obstacle because he faced it too; in his day, as in ours, Christianity was only one religion among many, and all of them were pressing their claims upon men's loyalties. Yet the Apostle writes with amazing boldness:

"Have this mind among yourselves, which you have in Christ Jesus, who, though he was in the form of God, did not count equality with God a thing to be grasped, but emptied himself, taking the form of a servant, being born in the likeness of men. And being found in human form he humbled himself and became obedient unto death, even death on a cross. Therefore God has highly exalted him and bestowed on him the name which is above every name, that at the name of Jesus every knee should bow, in heaven and on earth and under the earth, and every tongue confess that Jesus Christ is Lord, to the glory of God the Father . . ."

This is no brief for Christianity at the expense of other religious faiths. Paul knows that he is writing to Christians themselves, and he simply tells them to have the mind of Jesus Christ, the mind of perfect obedience to God. So far as they are concerned Jesus Christ is Lord, the highest they know, the One whom God has exalted and given a name above every name; therefore let them be subject to his Lordship and give him their obedience.

The challenge of other faiths really does not constitute more than an academic obstacle to Christian belief. A man asks, "What about Judaism or Islam or Hinduism?", but except in rare cases even the most anti-Christian Englishman would scarcely consider becoming a Jew or a Muslim or a Hindu. People brought up in Christian society have never migrated in large numbers to other ethnic faiths. It is not with Buddha or Mahomet or Confucius that Christ has to compete for men's allegiance in our Western world today, but with Karl Marx, Bertrand Russell and the American National Association of Manufacturers. There has emerged in recent years a new form of comparative religion presenting a far stronger challenge to the claims of Christianity than the great ethnic faiths of the Orient. It began with the Renaissance and gained momentum as modern man became drunk with a sense of his own power and importance. Humanism in its various forms, materialism, scientism, communism, a faith which dethrones God and sets man in God's place at the centre of the universe—there is the real challenge to Christianity, a challenge which has to be faced in our own lives. A man's religion concerns that thing in life, be it money or work or family or pleasure or prestige or socialism or pacifism, on which he pins his ultimate faith and to which he gives his ultimate loyalty, the thing on which he takes his stand, the thing about which he is committed. Paul speaks very sharply to our condition: "Jesus Christ is Lord. You do not have to prove his Lordship; God has done that. You are called to make certain that nothing usurps his Lordship in your own life, to give him your ultimate faith, your ultimate loyalty."

In that sense the other world religions *do* challenge us. They challenge the sheer formality, the lethargy, the insipidness of our Christian belief, the arrogance with which we try to defend Christ while at the same time failing to mani-

fest his spirit. One evening I had the high honour of chatting
for a few moments before an open fire with the Vice-President
(now President) of India, Servipelli Radhakrishnan. What
struck me about this charming and scholarly man was his
utter composure, his soul-quality. I recalled what he once
said to a Christian missionary, "You Christians seem to us
to be rather ordinary people making very extraordinary
claims." The missionary replied, "We make these claims not
for ourselves but for Jesus Christ." Radhakrishnan answered,
"If your Christ has not succeeded in making you into better
men and women, have we any reason to suppose that he
would do more for us if we became Christians?" It would be
stupid, would it not, to press the claims of Christianity on so
great and brilliant a man as Radhakrishnan, who probably
knows more about our faith than we do? Such a man
challenges us to be as true to the highest in Christianity as
he is to the highest in Hinduism, to give our faith the loyalty
and the intelligent understanding that other peoples give
to their faiths, and, if we really believe it the best, to obey it
rather than boast about it.

Many stories have been told about Bishop Lesslie
Newbigin, now on leave from South India, but the one
that appeals to me concerns an occasion when he preached
at the chapel in the University of Edinburgh. The students
had been invited to remain after the service and question
the speaker. One of them was very much a university
student. He said quite belligerently, "I didn't expect to
hear this provincial and narrow message from you, of
all people! You have seen so much of our world. You
have looked at the twentieth century from so many corners
of the room. Yet all you talked about was Christ. Why
Christ? Why didn't you bring us some insight from Mohammed? Why didn't you bring us some inspiration
from Buddha? Wouldn't that have been just as valid?" The
speaker looked at him with a disarming smile and said
quietly, "Oh, are you a Muslim?" "Why, no," answered
the lad. "Just as I thought," said the Bishop. "Mohammed is
not your problem. You are a Buddhist, then?" "Of course
not," snapped the boy. "Then I was right. Buddha is not
your problem. What are you?" "I don't know," the student
shifted uncomfortably, because this wasn't coming out at all
the way he had planned, "I suppose I'm supposed to be a

Christian." "Now isn't that amazing," concluded the Bishop. "I have never had that vague an answer from a Muslim. I have never had that vague an answer from a Buddhist. And I have lived and dealt with them for many years. You know, if I were you I shouldn't worry myself too much about their faith until I had made up my mind about Jesus Christ. Because it's easy to see, he's your problem."

Nothing could put the case more neatly, more charitably or more forcibly to the man who finds the challenge of other religions a trial to his faith. Our problem is not religion at all, our own or anyone else's, because Christ did not come, humanly-speaking, to found a religion. God founded the religion; Christ was obedient unto death. That is God's Word to us: Humble yourself. Make no claims for yourself or for Christianity, else you will prove that it is not the true faith but only a man-made religion become idolatrous. Do what Jesus did. Take the form of a servant. Be obedient. Then by faith you may open your lips and say with the Church in all the ages that Jesus Christ is Lord, to the glory of God the Father.

16

An Impossible Ideal

NOTHING frightens us more quickly than the prospect of some task or responsibility or ideal that seems impossible of fulfilment. A man comes away from a business interview. "Did you get the new job?" his wife asks him. "They offered it to me," he replies, "but I shall not accept it. They expect too much. You need to be more than human to measure up to all their demands. They will have to find someone more qualified and experienced. I should like to give it a try, but I just haven't got what it takes."

A great many people have exactly the same attitude toward the demands of Jesus. They are not antagonistic to the religion of Christ. If they stand outside the community of faith it is not because of their own pig-headed prejudices, but because they have looked seriously at the Faith and at what it implies for their own lives and they do not feel capable of measuring up to its demands. They are like that excellent young man in the Gospels, the Rich Young Ruler, who came to Jesus and asked to become a disciple, but when Jesus, after examining him morally, laid down the exacting conditions of discipleship, the young man shook his head sorrowfully and walked away.

Of all the obstacles that prevent some good people from moving forward to a complete and whole-hearted acceptance of Christianity there is none more formidable and discouraging than its sheer idealism. They read the New Testament and especially the teachings of Jesus in the Sermon on the Mount and they conclude that here is a code for angels, not for men. You would need to be more than human to measure up to its demands. This may be no arm-chair scepticism. Perhaps they have honestly tried to live the Christian life but have felt so lonely in their idealism and so wretched by the sense of failure, that they have simply given it up as hopeless. So now they begin to rationalize; they reason with themselves instead of with the facts. They say

173

something like this: "I am a fool to go on beating my head against a stone wall when nobody else is doing it. Why should I try to live for Christ in a world where other people live only for themselves? All honour to the man who can do it, but I haven't got what it takes."

Is it possible to be a Christian? With utmost candour we have to ask ourselves whether Christianity, set forth as a way of life in the New Testament, is in fact capable of being followed at all. We applaud the Sermon on the Mount, we admire its nobility and excellence, we acclaim it as the guide of perfect character and the blueprint of an ideal society, but as one man remarked about its teaching, "Most of us are not only *not* prepared to act like that, but we quite honestly don't think that we ought to act like that!" Looking at the Christian ethic with hard-headed realism, there is surely some doubt whether any man or group of men willing to take these lofty imperatives of purity, sincerity, magnanimity and charity, and put them into practice in the normal relationships of life, would survive long enough to serve the cause of Christ at all. Did Jesus intend that we should practise his teaching? Did he not rather intend it to inspire and challenge us like a kind of poetry, a symphonic dream, a beautiful piece of art, something to be looked at and admired but not taken literally? "You, therefore, must be perfect as your heavenly Father is perfect." Surely that call to angelic perfection were enough to remove the Christian ethic from the realm of practical possibility altogether.

I

We must consider, however, that when Jesus spoke to the disciples, *he* had no sense of confronting them with an impossible ideal. Like the manager of a firm who presents his new employees with the responsibilities of their position, so Jesus, when he invited men into the Kingdom of God, presented them with the rules of life in God's Kingdom. He was saying in effect, "If you would become my followers, this is how you must live"; and though, taken as a whole, the Sermon on the Mount may seem beyond our reach, yet broken down into its component parts, there is not a single injunction of which we can say categorically, "It will not work!" Brotherliness, cherishing no inward hate—that is difficult but liveable. Sincerity, our word as good as our bond—that also is liveable. Generosity performed without ostentation can be tried out in life; so can the teachings about marriage and divorce, about revenge and criticism, about prayer and faith. Would Jesus have concluded his sermon so specifically and emphatically if he had not expected his followers to begin there and then putting it into practice? He said, "Everyone who listens to these words of mine and acts upon them will be like a sensible man who built his home on rock. And everyone who listens to these words of mine and does not act upon them will be like a stupid man who built his house upon sand."

Worldly men sometimes have a patronizing habit of assuming that the religious teacher never knows what he is talking about, that somehow his very vocation insulates him against the real problems of real life in a real world. After the funeral of a wealthy business man some men were discussing the eulogy which had been rather fulsome in its praise of the finer qualities of the deceased. "We must not be too critical of the preacher," one man said indulgently, "he knew our friend only as a member of the Church; he didn't have to do business with him." We feel the same way about Jesus. We have no argument with his ethical teaching as such, but we think that we are more sophisticated than he was, that we know more about human nature than he knew; and human nature, being what it is, we do not believe that men are capable of practising that teaching. Men are naturally improvident, hence poverty in the world; naturally belligerent, hence wars; naturally selfish, hence cut-throat competition; naturally lustful, hence immorality. That is the human situation, and that is human nature in the raw —basically harsh, immoral, self-centred and incapable of change.

Exactly! But where did we get the idea that Jesus lived in starry-eyed ignorance of this situation? The Fourth Gospel has a telling verse about Jesus. Moffatt translates it, "He required no evidence from anyone about human nature. Well did he know what was in human nature." He had abundant reason to know. He knew that men could lie; they called him a glutton and a drunkard. He knew that men can be petty; they found fault with him for healing on the Sabbath. He knew that men can be cruel; they crucified him. The Master of men entertained no illusions about human nature; he knew its misery, but he also knew its grandeur; and if he made honouring claims and pitched his ideals high, it was only because he believed that men, despite their kinship with the dust, have the latent capacity to justify those claims and practise those ideals. Jesus believed that the weak could become strong and the crooked straight, that publicans and harlots could enter the Kingdom of God. Jesus looked into the faces of such men as ambitious, hot-tempered James and John, doubting Thomas and unstable Peter, moral pygmies such as we are, and he had the incredible faith to believe them capable of developing into giants. "You, therefore, shall be perfect . . ." It is indeed a code for angels, but Jesus believed with the Psalmist that we humans are just "a little lower than the angels".

II

We must also consider that Christianity as a way of life *has* been practised. We could dismiss the Christian ethic as impracticable if like other moral codes it had issued from the ivory tower of the philosophers. The Sermon on the Mount lays no claim to originality. You can find many of its precepts in the Old Testament and in the wisdom of the Greeks and Persians. What gives force to our Lord's teaching is the fact that *he* said it and that behind it stands his own life illustrating, enhancing and validating all that he said. Did he urge men to forgive their enemies? How ready he was to forgive. Did he enjoin them to be generous in their judgment of others? Was there ever a more magnanimous spirit than his? Not poetry, not a symphonic dream, not a piece of art, but a real, concrete philosophy of life tried and tested and found workable in the rough arena of human experience — the Teacher of Galilee offered *that* to men.

Is it possible to be a Christian? It depends on whether we answer the question from the viewpoint of our own pre-supposed limitations or from the viewpoint of what has actually happened in the world. A struggling artist might throw down his brush, stamp his feet in disgust and exclaim, "This kind of picture cannot be painted!", but let him step into an art gallery and he will see with his own eyes that the great masters have in fact painted such a picture. Art, music, science, engineering—these we judge not by our own fumbling efforts but by the highest that men have achieved; and whether or not we believe that Jesus was Divine, we must still acclaim his life as the highest achievement in human character. Christ is the Master of life. In him personality found its loftiest expression. He made of life altogether the most splendid thing ever to appear in this world. No one who comes face to face with the historic Jesus in the Gospels should doubt that there can be such a thing as human life lived on the basis of Christian teaching.

In *The Pilgrim's Progress,* when Christian and Hopeful came across Atheist, he asked where they were going. Christian replied, "We are going to Mount Sion." Atheist burst out laughing, "There is no such place as you dream of in all the world." But Hopeful knew better, "What, no Mount Sion? Did we not see from the Delectable Mountains the gate of the city?" We return that kind of answer to those who cynically tell us that Christianity is an ideal impossible to practise. We reply that we have seen it practised, not to perfection of course, but we have seen it as a genuine motivating philosophy of life in the character of men and women. We have seen it in politicians and in business and professional men, firm as steel and beautiful as music, who poured into this pagan world a Christlike integrity and humaneness that made spiritual life real. We have seen it in homes where children honoured their parents and parents respected their children, where religion was the master force and love dominated the fellowship. We have seen it in social movements that leaped high barricades, defied the scoffing of cynics and the fears of friends and opened the doors to new eras. The man who shrugs off the Sermon on the Mount and claims that it will not work faces the formidable task of revising the history books. He has to subtract from the story of mankind the biographies of all the saints, a magnificent tradition of unselfish devotion and service, and he has to find a plausible humanistic explanation to some of the best people of his own acquaintance and to some of the greatest men and women of our century.

A year ago the B.B.C. invited me to give a two-minute talk on the subject, "My Favourite Hero of the Twentieth Century". My friends all knew that I should choose Albert Schweitzer. He is one of those rare personalities that the human race produces only at long intervals, a genius who can excel in any profession that he chooses to follow. In his young manhood he had already distinguished himself as a scholar and a musician and was considered to be the world's leading interpreter of Bach's organ music. To the astonishment of his friends, this brilliant man, at the age of thirty, re-entered university to qualify himself as a medical doctor, and for the past fifty years he and his wife have been missionaries in French Equatorial Africa. Secluded from the civilized world, Schweitzer the genius should have faded into obscurity. Instead the world has gone to him. Men have visited Schweitzer at his jungle hospital in Lambaréné, and there they have seen the great doctor, still a profound thinker and brilliant musician, but spending himself utterly in the most incredibly primitive conditions to heal the bodies of Africans who sometimes neither understand nor appreciate him. Albert Schweitzer appeals to me as the hero of this century because he shows us that the path of true greatness still follows the footsteps of Christ; he shows us that Christianity as an ideal is possible of fulfilment.

III

Then we must consider that unless the Christian way of life is a *difficult* ideal, it is not an ideal at all. Repeatedly one encounters that truth in the poetry of Robert Browning. When they buried the Grammarian they eulogized one who had found life's meaning not in success but in aspiration, not in achievement but in striving.

> "That low man seeks a little thing to do,
>   Sees it and does it.
> This high man with a great thing to pursue,
>   Dies ere he knows it."

In contrast, Andrea del Sarto, the perfect painter, discovered that the spark of life dies when one feels that he has reached the pinnacle of excellence.

> "A man's reach should exceed his grasp
>   Or what's a heaven for?"

So the Sermon on the Mount seems impossible of fulfilment by mere humans! Do you think it would have survived

178

as a timeless statement of ethical principles if every Tom, Dick and Harry could keep it as easily as they keep out of jail? Would it be worthy of the Master of men that he should point his followers to a way of life less demanding than that which he himself incarnated? "You, therefore, must be perfect as your heavenly Father is perfect." Is it not this very standard of Divine perfection that gives the Christian life its persistent fascination, that stimulates us, challenges us, preserves us from complacency and beckons us like a shining mountain peak to new heights of character?

Stanley Jones once said to Mahatma Gandhi, "I am very anxious to see Christianity nationalized in India, so that it shall no longer be a foreign thing identified with a foreign people and a foreign government but part of the national life of India, contributing to India's uplift and redemption. What would you suggest that we do to make that possible?" Gandhi replied, "I would suggest, first, that all of you Christians begin to live more like Jesus Christ. Second, I would suggest that you practise your religion without toning it down. Third, I would suggest that you put your emphasis on love, for love is the centre and soul of Christianity." We are constantly hearing from missionaries and government representatives abroad what a great admiration intelligent non-Christians in other parts of the world have for the teachings and character of Jesus. *They* do not consider Christianity an impossible ideal; they acknowledge the Sermon on the Mount as the noblest and most challenging way of life ever presented to man; and if they do not take Christ's way of life seriously, it is only because they have never seen it taken seriously by people who profess to believe in Christ. Why should they do what we have not the courage to do? Why should they aspire to the heights of Christian character when we, who are unwilling that our reach should exceed our grasp, settle for something less costly and demanding, thereby losing the dynamic of a great ideal?

When Abraham Lincoln died, Tolstoy looking across from Russia, said, "He was a bit of Christ." George Whitefield said of Isaac Watts, "He was Christ in miniature." After the death of Sir William Osler a cousin wrote, "My intimate association with him as guide, philosopher and friend leads me to the belief that he was of all men the most Christlike in his life and the most Godlike in his attributes."

Concerning Dr. Edward Wilson, who perished on Scott's expedition to the Antarctic, a man named Pennell later wrote to Dr. Wilson's widow, "I never thought the Christ-life possible as an ideal until I saw it in your husband." These were not all pious men; in some cases they had little to say about their religion; but when their contemporaries sought some ideal that would express their magnificent integrity and unselfishness they could only point to the character of Christ. Christ is still the highest we know, and the highest we can say about any man is still to compare him with Christ. That does not make Christianity an impossible ideal; rather it makes Christianity the worthiest, most challenging goal toward which in this life we can strive.

IV

It is most important to consider that while Jesus pointed his followers to seemingly impossible standards, he did not expect his followers to achieve them in their own strength. A man will say, "I do not accept Christ as the Son of God, but I do accept him as a moral teacher"; and yet if Christ were no more than a moral teacher, we should not have constructed theologies about him and erected churches to his glory. There have been many moral teachers in history, and their teachings now gather dust in morality's museum. Why? Because they did not contain the power of their own fulfil-ment; they showed man the right way to live, then left him to his own resources; they were like a noble sword placed in hands too feeble to lift it. That is what prompts our scepti-cism and forces the question, "Is it possible to be a Christian?"; not that we doubt the validity of our Lord's teaching or even the capacity of human nature, as such, to fulfil it, but we know ourselves, we know that "the heart is deceitful above all things", that we have noble intentions but not the will to carry them out. The Apostle Paul voiced our predicament when he said, "I can will what is right, but I cannot do it."

Let us interject one consideration here, namely, that we may have allowed the sheer magnitude of the Christian ethic to overwhelm us. Taken as a whole the Sermon on the Mount does seem like a code, if not for angels, at least for supermen, and when the entire avalanche of its demands falls on our conscience, we simply collapse with discouragement. We forget that a very important element in the Christian life is the element of growth. Just as we cannot swallow the whole body of Christian doctrine in one gulp, neither shall we reach the Christian ideal of moral perfection in one bound. No more than we expect a school child to master the entire curriculum on his first day at school, does Jesus expect us to master all the rules of his Kingdom when first we accept his invitation to enter it. Christ expects only that we shall be obedient to him and that we shall act and react to each situation as it arises in a manner consistent with his will and teaching as we understand them. There are times when we shall succeed and times when we shall fail, but by God's grace we shall learn from both our successes and our failures and we shall make them stepping-stones to higher achievement.

Even more fundamentally we make the mistake of *beginning* our Christianity at the wrong place. Being a Christian means more than setting oneself in a rather systematic way to follow the teachings of Jesus. It is a form of self-salvation and therefore idolatrous to construct a religion based exclusively on those teachings. Many people try to do it, like that man who says, "I do not accept Christ as the Son of God. I am not a mystic. I don't pray. I don't go to church. But I do believe in the teaching of Jesus." The most obvious thing we can say to that man is, "Why not exemplify those teachings to a greater extent than you do?" The demand is meaningless, however, just as meaningless as expecting some strange child to enter your home and give you the same spontaneous respect and obedience that come naturally from your own children. Your children obey you because they love you, and they love you because you first loved them. First comes your love, then their obedience. Indeed your love makes possible their obedience, because it awakens their gratitude, kindles their sense of shame when they fail you, but at the same time removes their fear because they know you will forgive them, and quickens their resolve to please you in the future. The religion of Jesus begins there—not with a code of demands but with a relationship to God, a sense of being at home with God and of being loved by God that makes possible our obedience to his demands.

One of the great Chinese Christian leaders in modern times was T. Z. Koo. Dr. Koo has often told what won him to Christianity in his student days. It was simply that Christianity came to him with a proposition different from that offered by any other religion. Confucianism, in which he grew up, was concerned only with ethics, only with the right and wrong of things, but Dr. Koo says that he never found any peace or joy by simply trying to be a good man; indeed the persistent sense of failure only made him wretched. Then one day a missionary told him that if he would open his heart to a Personality, the ethical programme would follow. Dr. Koo responded. He became a Christian. He took Christ into his life, and the problem of morality ceased to torment him. He now stood in a new relationship to God where the old plodding, discouraging cry, "I ought" and "I must" was changed to the redeeming and glorious "I can" and "I will". To the man empowered by Christ unto salvation all things enter the realm of moral possibility, even the perfect character of God himself.

17

Belief is Commitment

THE Danish theologian, Kierkegaard, related a homely
parable about a flock of geese that milled around in a
filthy barnyard imprisoned by a high wooden fence. One
day a preaching goose came into their midst. He stood on an
old crate and admonished the geese for being content with
this confined, earthbound existence. He recounted the
exploits of their forefathers who spread their wings and flew
the trackless wastes of the sky. He spoke of the goodness of
the Creator who had given geese the urge to migrate and the
wings to fly. This pleased the geese. They nodded their
heads and marvelled at these things and applauded the
eloquence of the preaching goose. All this they did. But one
thing they never did; they did not fly. They went back to
their waiting dinner, for the corn was good and the barnyard
secure.

We bring to a close this book on "Barriers to Christian
Belief". There are such barriers, to be sure, high fences that
block our vision and prevent us from moving forward to a
complete and whole-hearted acceptance of the Christian
Faith. We shall not be convinced about the illusoriness of
these barriers, however, until we *decide* to spread our wings
and fly over them. The biggest obstacle to Christian belief
does not lie in some thorny theological issue, nor yet in some
burning practical issue, but in our own timidity and in-
decisiveness. If we are not Christians, it is not because our
religious questions remain unanswered, but because we
cannot reach a decision, we cannot make up our minds to
follow Jesus Christ.

No one has spoken more relevantly to the current mood
of scepticism than has J. H. Oldham in his excellent book,
Life is Commitment. Dr. Oldham is keenly aware that the
Church has lost contact with many of the ablest and finest
people in our society, and with infinite respect for these
people he addresses himself to them in the attempt to find a

183

common meeting-ground between religion and other expressions of our culture. At the very outset Dr. Oldham states frankly that religion differs radically from other forms of knowledge in that it cannot be approached by the academic high-road alone. No man can reason himself into the Kingdom of God. "There are some things in life—," writes Dr. Oldham, "and they may be the most important things— that we cannot know by research or reflection, but only by committing ourselves. We must dare in order to know." Again he says, "Life is full of situations to which I can respond not with part of myself but only with the commitment of my whole being."[1]

I

Enlarging upon this thought, we must consider, first, that no person, however extensively he reads or travels, will ever reach a place where *all* his doubts have been cleared away. I recall two men who were so serious in their quest of the truth about Jesus Christ that one purchased an expensive theological library and the other made a pilgrimage to the Holy Land, yet neither felt himself any closer to the object of his search. We picture as the ideal result of this book some young person saying gratefully, "My questions have been answered. The obstacles in my path have been removed. Now I can move forward to a complete and whole-hearted acceptance of Christianity." It does not work out that way, however, simply because the Christian life does not take us across a level plain but up a mountain side. There are always new gulleys to be crossed and new peaks to be conquered. The stream of life which bears us along will not stay until knowledge is complete. Somewhere we have to live and act on the basis of such limited knowledge as we possess.

In his amusing little story, "The Retroactive Existence of Mr. Juggins", Stephen Leacock parodied the elaborate preparations that sometimes precede marriage. Mr. Juggins had fallen in love and really intended to marry the girl, but he was not the kind to rush into marriage without first preparing for this important step. So he went into moral training by teaching a Sunday School class. Soon, however, he

[1] J. H. Oldham, *Life is Commitment* (Student Christian Movement Press Ltd., London, 1953), p. 24.

realized that in order to be an effective teacher he needed to undertake a serious study of the history of Palestine. But then he felt he would be a cad to force his intentions on a girl while only partially acquainted with Israelitish history, so he stayed away from her for two years until he felt really fit to propose. Of course, by the time he had pronounced himself ready she was married to a man who didn't know Moses from Ahab.

As Dr. Oldham pointed out, there are some things in life which we cannot know except by committing ourselves, and married love is one of them. It is a rare young man who prior to marriage reaches a point where he can be one hundred per cent certain that his fiancée is exactly the girl whom he ought to choose for his wife. Even the most devoted couple entertain doubts about each other, but if they keep postponing their wedding until all their doubts have been dispelled, they will have nothing to look forward to but a very long engagement. Men and women who wish to be absolutely and categorically certain of their compatibility outside marriage are demanding the impossible. Only within marriage do we discover true married love. We must dare in order to know.

That makes sense because marriage involves persons, and you can never know a person save in some measure of commitment to him. The Christian religion also involves a Person. "I know *whom* I have believed," wrote Paul to Timothy. At no point in the New Testament do you find Christianity set forth as a full-blown theological system which you must accept in its entirety before you can call yourself a Christian. Jesus summoned men not to a system of religious faith but to an act of personal commitment. "Follow me," he said to the disciples by the seashore; and even when they had followed him throughout his ministry and felt the impact of his personality and witnessed his miracles and listened to his teaching, even then he made it very clear to them that they still had a great deal to learn; they would still encounter obstacles to their faith, but by the help of his Spirit they would be able to overcome these obstacles. The man who honestly longs for certitude in the Christian life will find it only in an act of commitment to Jesus Christ.

Then we must consider that even if a person by sheer reasoning power does reach a point of academic conviction, that will not suffice to make him a Christian. In the twelfth chapter of Mark's Gospel we find the very interesting case of a man who agreed with Jesus absolutely. The incident took place in the Temple during the last week of our Lord's earthly life on that day when his enemies tried to trap him with a series of difficult questions. With more sincerity than malevolence one scribe asked him, "What commandment is the first of all?" Jesus gave the classic reply that above all else we are required to love God and our neighbour. "You are right, Teacher," said the scribe, reiterating this summary of the law; and the Gospel writer tells us that "when Jesus saw that he had answered wisely, he said to him, 'You are not far from the Kingdom of God.' "

"Not far from the Kingdom"—it was a tremendous compliment that Jesus paid to this man who did not belong to the apostolic group, as indeed he pays it to many people today who stand outside the orthodox community of faith, people who, making no profession of Christianity, agree with the essential philosophy of Christ. At the same time, Jesus left no doubt that the man did stand outside the Kingdom. He was not a Christian even though he agreed with Christ. The disciples, Peter, Andrew, James and John, might envy the intellectual certitude of this Jewish scribe, but they possessed what he did not possess—a spiritual certitude. They knew Christ as the outsider could never know him, because they had made a decision for Christ. They had not waited until their knowledge of Christ was complete but had committed their lives to him on the basis of what they did know, and their act of commitment brought them inside the Kingdom.

No man ever learns to swim by reading books of instruction, nor does he learn by clinging to the edge of a pool or by splashing about in two feet of water. His career as a swimmer begins only on the day when he takes the initial plunge into deep water and launches out, trusting the water to hold him up. There was a paratrooper in the Second World War who said, "The first time I leaped out of a plane everything within me resisted. I had listened to lectures, I had mastered the techniques of using a parachute, I had practised jumping under simulated conditions, but still I did not believe that this frail piece of silk could actually hold me up." Then he said, "Nothing in this world compares with the thrill I experienced when I leaped into the sky, pulled the cord and found that the whole thing was actually true, that the parachute would support me and take me safely to the ground."

Christian experience begins in the same way. A man enters the Kingdom of God, which is another way of saying that he comes to an inside knowledge of Christian truth and therefore to a place of Christian certitude, only when he takes the plunge of belief, a leap of faith in a great act of commitment to Jesus Christ. Thomas à Kempis expressed it like this: "When one that was in anxiety of mind, often wavering between fear and hope, did once, being oppressed with grief, humbly prostrate himself in church before the altar in prayer, and said within himself, 'Oh, if I knew that I should yet persevere!', he presently heard within him an answer from God which said, 'If thou didst know it, what wouldst thou do? Do now what thou wouldst do then, and thou shalt be secure . . .'" It is a daring faith that we proclaim in the historic creed: "I believe in God the Father Almighty, Maker of Heaven and earth, and in Jesus Christ, his only Son our Lord . . ." a daring faith about which we could argue interminably, but we shall never discover its truth until we live and act as if it *were* true and stake our very lives on its power to support us.

One of the most searching addresses at the Second Assembly of the World Council of Churches was that delivered by Charles Malik, a distinguished Arab statesman and an Orthodox lay delegate from Lebanon. "My brethren," he said, "a common faith unites us. We believe in God . . . We most certainly believe in Jesus Christ . . . We assuredly believe in the Holy Ghost, the Holy Catholic Church, the Communion of Saints, the Forgiveness of Sins, the Resurrection of the Body and the Life Everlasting." Whereupon Dr. Malik launched into a frank and penetrating analysis of the responsibility of Christian nations and Christian individuals to the great political, social and moral issues of our day. Dr. Malik was saying that what we *believe* means very little; what we *believe in* means everything. And if we believe in the great Christian verities, then our belief will express itself in the commitment of our whole being; we shall live and act and labour and serve as if the Christian faith were true.

III

Let us approach our question from another angle and consider that every man has to discover the truth of Christianity for himself. Some things in life can be borrowed — umbrellas, for example, as everyone knows who has shared in the "brolly" exchange in cloakrooms and railway carriages. To some extent academic knowledge and technical skills can be communicated from one generation to another, and parents can pass on to their children a certain business sense and a love of culture. Religion is different, however. You can teach a person the facts of religion, you can instruct him in the content of the Bible, the subject matter of Christian doctrine, the history of the Church, the philosophy of religion. All of this he can borrow from you second-hand. He cannot borrow your religious experience, your first-hand knowledge of God. This he must discover for himself in a personal act of commitment.

So declares the writer of the thirty-fourth Psalm, a man possessed by one overwhelming and transcendent truth — the goodness of God. He sings about that goodness and the quality of life which it produces in all who take it seriously. His Psalm begins with an outburst of praise : "I will bless the Lord at all times. His praise shall continually be in my mouth." He summons us to join him, "O magnify the Lord with me and let us exalt his name together." As a proof of God's goodness the Hebrew poet points to his own experience, "I sought the Lord and he answered me and delivered me from all my fears." God's goodness has been confirmed in the experience of other men, "That poor man cried, and the Lord heard him and saved him out of his troubles." The Psalmist would not have us take his word for it, however, or the word of other people. He knows that we shall never believe in the goodness of God until we put it to the test and assimilate it into our own lives. "O taste and see that the Lord is good."

188

Taste differs radically from the other four senses. Someone tells you about the flavour and the nutritive quality of a certain kind of food. You hear about this food, you see it, you smell it and you touch it, but you still have to taste the food before it will do you any good and satisfy your deepest hungers. Some people apply to religion only the sense of hearing. They listen to sermons, they enjoy theological discussions, but they never enter the Kingdom of God because they bog down in pious verbiage. Others apply only the sight, viewing religion detachedly as they would a painting, going to public worship as spectators and admiring the example of Christian character without making the effort to emulate it. Others simply smell religion. They pass the church each day on their way to work as they do a bakery, sensitive to the rather pleasant aroma surrounding Christianity but admitting neither the time nor the inclination to enter and make a purchase. Some touch religion, gingerly perhaps, as they might touch a freshly-painted chair; they handle the Bible, they occupy a church pew, at the same time making certain that God never comes closer than arm's length to the heart. Figuratively we can apply to religion the senses of hearing, sight, smell and touch without their making the slightest appreciable difference in our lives. Only the fifth sense, the sense of taste, the act of commitment which assimilates religion and puts it to the test, only this will satisfy our spiritual hungers.

To know the truth of religion you have to taste it, which means that you have to stop arguing about it and begin practising it. The late John R. Mott, a layman, who was the first Honorary President of the World Council of Churches, said that in his early years at university he began to doubt the efficacy of prayer. He found it difficult to believe that prayer could change either events or persons; it seemed impossible to him that in answer to man's petitions God should contravene his own scientifically-established laws. To deal with his doubts Mott decided to read some books on prayer. He read forty-three. He found them helpful and inspiring, but they did not resolve his doubts. At last he decided to try a different approach. He stopped reading and abandoned his wearisome discussions on prayer and actually began to pray. He prayed regularly and earnestly and soon he discovered the value of prayer.

Years ago a popular magazine published an inspiring article called "The Day that Changed a Life". It was a true story about a girl whose influence so elevated the atmosphere of the office in which she worked that her employer asked her the secret of it. She told him that several months previously she had made up her mind to live one complete day as if there really were a God who loves us and cares for us and judges us and guides us. She had always believed in the belief in God, but this day she would live as though that belief were true. It had made such a difference to her, to the way she worked and approached other people and dealt with her problems, that she continued the experiment a second day and a third, and now she felt God "closer than breathing and nearer than hands and feet". Previously she had been a Christian only by hearsay; now she was a Christian by vital apprehension and insight. By making a great act of personal commitment she had made religious experience her own; she had passed from a second-hand knowledge about God to a first-hand knowledge of God himself.

IV

This brings us to consider, finally, that in religion we are not asked to make up our minds; we are asked to make up our lives. Here we cannot escape the necessity of decision. A man will say, "I shall not become a Christian because there are too many obstacles in the path of belief, too many questions that have not yet been answered to my satisfaction. I am not an atheist. I do not deny the existence of God, but neither am I convinced that God does exist. Therefore I shall withhold my judgment and explore the whole question more thoroughly." We respect this man's honesty and we shall not attempt to force him to a decision. Obviously he must make up his own mind. Let him understand, however, that time does not stand still while he weighs the pros and cons of religious truth. The stream moves forward, and though we refuse to make up our minds, we cannot refuse to make up our lives. They get made up one way or the other.

However we may deplore Communism, at least the Marxists do not make a virtue of neutrality. Speaking at the United Nations General Assembly in October 1961, the Nationalist Chinese Foreign Minister quoted from the Peking "New Terminology Dictionary" which defines the term "Neutralist line" as follows: "A day-dream that can never be realized. Even its theory is not correct. As the world situation stands today there are only two roads—either to support capitalism or to support socialism—and there is no third road. Any vain hope to take on a third road is doomed to failure." Such a statement should be compulsory reading for those Western politicians and labour leaders who publish their romantic notions about leading the uncommitted countries. Uncommitted to what? we ask. Uncommitted to end the political slavery that oppresses men and shoots them in the back when they try to cross a border? Uncommitted to resist imperialist aggression that gobbles up small countries and emasculates them in the name of "freedom"? Uncommitted to oppose the tyranny that imprisons distinguished intellectuals, sensitive artists and courageous churchmen, brainwashes them and liquidates them because they think of themselves as individuals with minds of their own? We do not hear the Marxists talking about being uncommitted. They are precisely committed, and so are all men, if they face the truth honestly. We may refuse to make up our minds, but our lives get made up one way or the other.

Two ways of life confront mankind in the world today, and the way we follow decides our answer to questions such as these: Does life make sense or is it simply nonsense? Is life a meaningless struggle or is it nurtured in the purpose and goodness of Almighty God? Are we insects with no more significance than a fly on a window-pane, or are we the children of a wise and loving Father? Are the love and kindness and generosity which we show in our finest hours indications of the true nature of life, or are they just so much sentimental weakness? What is more important— people or things, individuals or institutions? Do governments exist to be served by us or do they exist to serve? Is God, or is he not? Was Jesus a dreamer and a psychopathic fool, or did he know how life at its best should be lived? It does not require the removal of any obstacles before we can answer these basic and ultimate questions. We answer them in spite of ourselves. Whatever we believe with our minds, our lives

191

are committed either to God's way or to the God-denying way, and all that matters in religion is the act of commitment.

The dramatic turning-point in our Lord's earthly career, so carefully reported by three of the Gospel writers, occurs while Jesus and the disciples are walking along the road to Caesarea Philippi. This is the occasion of Peter's momentous confession, "Thou art the Christ, the Son of the living God," a spiritual insight so profound that, according to Jesus, it could have come only by inspiration of God himself. Notice how Mark begins his account, ". . . and *on the way* he asked his disciples . . ." a phrase which denotes something larger than a country road in Palestine. "On the way", Christ's way, men have always discerned the truth about God. The deepest insights have come to them not in their comfortable ivory towers of philosophical and mystical speculation but on the rough road of Christian obedience and service. The great believers in Christ have always been the great followers of Christ. Their minds may have held reservations, but their lives were precisely committed to his way, and in the act of commitment they received from God a spiritual discernment equal to any obstacles.

So ends this book in which we have attempted to grapple with some of the practical and theoretical barriers that deter many good people from an acceptance of the Christian Faith. The book has to end, because there are limits to which theological argument can go. No person by sheer academic reasoning will ever reach a place where *all* his doubts have been cleared away, and even if by some miracle he did achieve this, it would not suffice to make him a Christian. Christianity is a way of life. It must be seen from the inside. It must be lived in order to be understood. It cannot be borrowed second-hand from the pages of a book but has to be discovered first-hand in a radical act of commitment to Jesus Christ. "There are some things in life — and they may be the most important things — that we cannot know by research or reflection, but only by committing ourselves. We must dare in order to know." The fences, the obstacles, are there and will remain there until we *decide* to spread our wings and fly over them.